CATALOGUE OF THE COINS

IN THE

PRINCE OF WALES MUSEUM

OF

WESTERN INDIA, BOMBAY

CATALOGUE OF THE COINS

IN THE

PRINCE OF WALES MUSEUM

OF

WESTERN INDIA, BOMBAY

THE SULTANS OF GUJARAT

COMPILED BY

C. R. SINGHAL, Gallery Assistant

EDITED BY

G. V. ACHARYA, B.A., M.R.A.S., Curator, Archæological Section

هرکرا روی و رواجے هست بر سطح زمین
سکۀ اقبالِ شاهِ هند دارد بر جبین

Whoever possesses name and fame on the surface of the earth bears on his forehead the stamp of the glory of the Sovereign of India

Munshiram Manoharlal Publishers Pvt. Ltd.

ISBN 81-215-0247-0
9 788121 502474
ISB

Reprinted 1988
First published in 1935

Published by Munshiram Manoharlal Publishers Private Limited,
Post Box no. 5715, 54 Rani Jhansi Road, New Delhi-110055,
printed by Gayatri Offset Press, A-66, Sector-2, NOIDA-201 301.

PREFACE.

In the year 1923 a big hoard of the copper coins of Gujarat sultans was found from a hill near Marole, a village to the north-east of Andheri Station of the B.B. & C.I. Railway, Thana District. About a hundred coins, mostly of unknown types, were selected for this museum, about 345 coins were distributed to other museums, and the rest returned to the Victoria and Albert Museum, Bombay.

Seven years after this, the picked collection of the late Dr. G. P. Taylor, consisting of 179 silver and 459 copper coins, was purchased from Mr. S. M. Contractor of Bombay. Again in 1932 Professor S. H. Hodivala, M.A., offered his whole collection of coins to the museum, including 137 silver and 874 copper coins of the Gujarat sultans. The Trustees availed themselves of this opportunity of enriching their collection of these coins, and it is but natural that Mr. A. Master, I.C.S., C.I.E., the President of the Numismatic Society of India, advised them, in his presidential address for the year 1932, to undertake the publication of a catalogue of these coins. The examination and registration of the coins in these collections gave Mr. Singhal, my Gallery Assistant, an opportunity to specialise and qualify himself as the proper man to compile this catalogue. From the total number of about 500 silver and 2,000 copper coins about 1,000 typical coins are incorporated in this catalogue and about 150 selected ones are illustrated in the plates. It is rather unfortunate that, though about 20 gold coins of this dynasty are known, this museum has secured only one specimen so far.

With a view, however, to make the catalogue as exhaustive and representative as possible, members of the Numismatic Society of India and various collectors and museums—both in and out of India—were requested to favour us with a list of such of their Gujarat sultan coins as have not been catalogued so far. With the help of several replies, lists, and photographs received in response to our appeal it was possible to include in this catalogue the description of such additional coins as are not in our cabinet. These coins are described in chronological order, and bear the additional letters a, b, c, etc. along with the serial numbers. We take this opportunity of expressing our heart-felt thanks to all those who have extended their healthy co-operation to us in this work.

The first serious attempt at describing these coins was made by Dr. G. P. Taylor in 1902 in his scholarly paper printed in the *Journal of the Bombay Branch of the Royal Asiatic Society*. In 1907 Mr. H. N. Wright described coins of this dynasty in his volume II of *The Indian Museum Coins*. During the course of these thirty years several new types have come to light. In 1926 Professor S. H. Hodivala published his paper on some unpublished coins in the *Bombay Asiatic Society's Journal*, New Series, volume II. In compiling this catalogue, these publications, as well as other stray lists and notes written on several coins by Messrs. Edward Thomas, Lane-Poole, E. Oliver, A. Master, C. R. Singhal, A. Botham, and K. N. Dikshit were consulted, and we thank them heartily for the help we received from their publications.

G. V. ACHARYA,
Curator.

LIST OF CONTENTS.

LIST OF PLATES.

LIST OF ABBREVIATIONS.

Ahmadi	..	Mirat-i-Ahmadi, translated by Mr. Bird.
A.N.S. ..	..	List of Coins with the American Numismatic Society of New York, U.S.A.
B.B.R.A.S.	..	Bombay Branch Royal Asiatic Society.
B.M.C. ..	..	Catalogue of Indian Coins in the British Museum: The Muhammadan States, by Stanley Lane-Poole, 1885.
Ferishta ..	..	History of the Rise of the Mahomedan Power, by John Briggs, vol. IV.
Gad. Coll.	..	Mr. R. H. Gadgil's Collection of Coins.
Hodivala	..	The Unpublished Coins of the Gujarat Sultanat, by S. H. Hodivala, J.B.B.R.A.S. (N.S.), vol. II, p. 19, 1926.
I.M.C. II	..	Catalogue of the Coins in the Indian Museum, Calcutta, vol. II, by H. N. Wright, 1907.
J.A.S.B.	..	Journal of the Asiatic Society of Bengal.
N.C. ..	..	Numismatic Chronicle.
N.S. ..	..	Numismatic Supplement.
O. ..	..	Mr. E. E. Oliver's Article in J.A.S.B., vol. LVIII, p. 1, for 1889.
P.C.C.A...	..	Catalogue of the Provincial Coin Cabinet, Assam, by A. W. Botham, 1930.
P.M.L. ..	..	Provincial Museum, Lucknow.
P.P.M.R.	..	Phayre Provincial Museum, Rangoon.
Sikandari	..	Mirat-i-Sikandari, translated by Fazlullah.
Taylor ..	..	Coins of the Gujarat Sultanat, by G. P. Taylor, J.B.B.R.A.S., vol. XXI, p. 278, 1902.
Thomas ..	..	The Chronicles of the Pathan Kings of Delhi, by Edward Thomas, 1871.
W.M.R. ..	..	Watson Museum of Antiquities, Rajkot.

GENEALOGICAL TABLE OF THE KINGS OF THE GUJARAT SALTANAT.

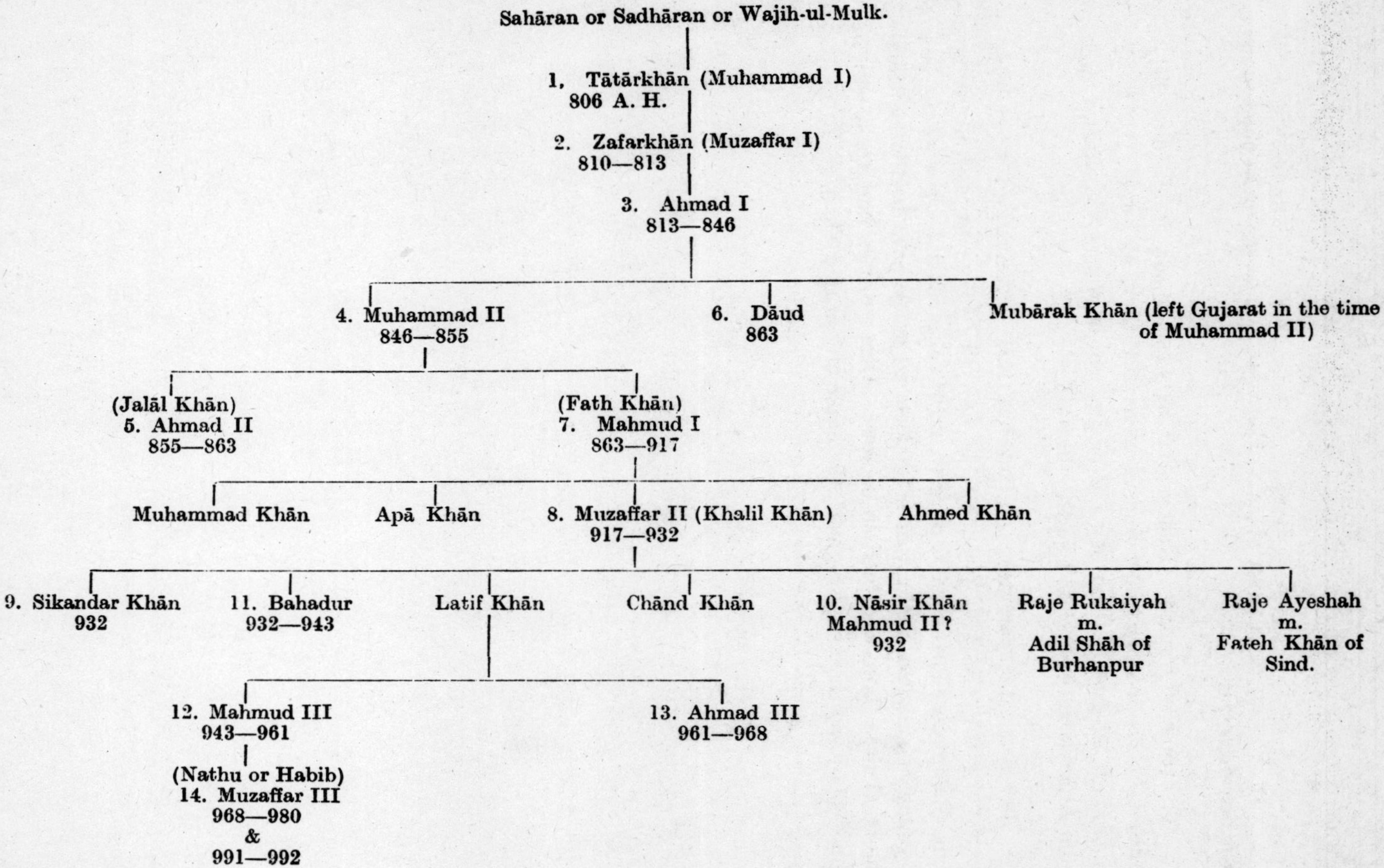

NOTES.

The relation of Ahmad III and Muzaffar III, as given in the following table, is rather doubtful.

The coins of Ahmad III show that he was the son of Mahmud III, while the authors of *Mirat-i-Sikandari* and *Ahmadi* say that, Mahmud III, having left no male issue, Ahmed III, son of Latif Khan, who was only a small boy, was brought from Ahmedabad and seated on the throne.

As regards the parentage of Muzaffar III, Ferishta and Abul Fazal and the author of *Mirat-i-Ahmadi* relate that, as Etimad Khan, who was all powerful at the time, did not consider any near relative of the sultan as fit for governing, he produced a young boy named Nathu whom he declared on oath to be the legitimate son of the late sultan, born and bred in secrecy. Other nobles had to accept his story, and the boy was declared king with the name of Muzaffar Shah.

CHRONOLOGICAL LIST OF THE KINGS OF THE GUJARAT SULTANAT.

No.	Name of King.	Year of Birth.	Reign.
1	Muhammad I	..	A.H. 806 (A.D. 1403).
2	Muzaffar I	A.H. 743 (A.D. 1342) ..	A.H. 810-813 (A.D.1407-1410).
3	Ahmad I	A.H. 793 (A.D. 1391) ..	A.H. 813-846 (A.D. 1410-1442).
4	Muhammad II ..	..	A.H. 846-855 (A.D. 1442-1451).
5	Qutb-ud-din Ahmad II	*Circ.* A.H. 805 (A.D.1402)	A.H. 855-863 (A.D. 1451-1458).
6	Daud	..	A.H. 863 (A.D. 1458).
7	Mahmud I	A.H. 849 (A.D. 1445) ..	A.H. 863-917 (A.D. 1459-1511).
8	Muzaffar II	A.H. 880 (A.D. 1475) ..	A.H. 917-932. (A.D. 1511-1525).
9	Sikandar	..	A.H. 932 (A.D. 1525).
10	Mahmud II	*Circ.* A.H. 926 (A.D. 1519)	A.H. 932 (A.D. 1525).
11	Bahadur	A.H. 912 (A.D. 1506) ..	A.H. 932-943 (A.D. 1526-1536).
12	Mahmud III	A.H. 932 (A.D. 1525) ..	A.H. 943-961) (A.D. 1536-1553).
13	Ahmad III	..	A.H. 961-968) (A.D. 1553-1560).
14	Muzaffar III	..	A.H. 968-980 (A.D. 1560-1573) and A.H. 991-992 (A.D. 1583-1584).

Notes :—

1. THE dates in the foregoing list have been entered after weighing all the available information, but absolute correctness is difficult to obtain because the authorities themselves differ in so many places.

The following are the important discrepancies :—

(*a*) According to Ferishta, Muzaffar I died in 814, but the detailed account in *Mirat-i-Sikandari* of the death of Muzaffar I in 813 being poisoned by his grandson, Ahmad I, disproves the statement of Farishta.

(*b*) According to *Mirat-i-Sikandari* and *Ahmadi*, Ahmad I is considered to have died in 845. The copper coins of this sultan in the museum collection bear the last date A.H. 846. This corroborates the statement in *Tabaqat-i-Akbari* that Ahmad's successor, Muhammad II, ascended, the throne on ' ' 3rd Rabi-al-Akhar, 846."

(*c*) Ferishta describes Ahmad II as born in 855, and as ascending the throne in the 49th year of his age; but, according to other histories, he is taken to have ascended the throne in A.H. 855.

(*d*) According to *Mirat-i-Sikandari* and *Ahmadi*, Muzaffar II was born in 880, and ascended the throne in 917 in the 27th year of his age; but Farishta says that he was born in 875 and came to the throne in the 41st year of his age. If the year of birth of the former authorities is to be admitted, he ought to have ascended the throne in the 37th year of his age, and not in the 27th. If he was born in 875, the statement of Ferishta about the date of accession seems to be correct.

(*e*) According to *Mirat-i-Sikandri* and *Ahmadi*, Mahmud III ascended the throne in 943; but, according to *Ferishta* and *Tabaqat-Akbari*, in 944. The earliest coin in the collection bears the date 944. The correct time therefore may probably be the end of A.H. 943.

(*f*) According to *Mirat-i-Sikandari* and *Ahmadi*, Ahmad III died in 968; but, according to *Ferishta*, he died in A.H. 969. The coins of Muzaffar III, the successor of Ahmad III, dated 968 are known, which substantiate the former statements.

2. The coins of all the eleven sultans out of fourteen, *i.e.*, excepting those of Muhammad I, Daud, and Sikandar, are included in this catalogue. As these three sultans were on the throne for a very short period, and as they were either deposed or murdered before they could establish themselves, it is not possible to get their coins.

3. (*a*) Four dateless copper coins issued in the name of Nasir Shah are attributed to Mahmud II, whose original name was Nasir Khan. They are undoubtedly of Gujarat fabric.

(*b*) *Ferishta's* reference to coins issued in the name of Muhammad Shah Farooky, nephew of Bahadur Shah, is not so reliable. Both *Mirat-i-Sikandari* and *Ahmadi* say with one voice that, as soon as Muhammad Shah heard the sad news of his uncle Bahadur's death, he was so much grieved that he stopped talking to anybody and resigned his life a few days after the death of Sultan Bahadur.

(*c*) In the *British Museum Catalogue of Coins of Muhammadan States* three copper coins, Nos. 437, 438, and 439, are doubtfully assigned to Muhammad Shah, the Pretender. But now it is admitted that these coins were really struck by Kadir Shah (Mahmud III of Gujarat) of Malwa, vide article by Mr. H. N. Wright in *Numismatic Chronicle*, volume XII, 1932, page 31.

INTRODUCTION.

GENERAL.

A CRITICAL study of the history of India shows that there has always been a succession of rise and fall of the central power, with consequent changes, in the inverse order, in the positions of the provincial rulers. Whenever the emperor at Delhi was a powerful monarch, he reduced all the rulers in different parts of India to mere feudal kings, or independently appointed governors of his own choice and had a guiding hand in the administration of the various provinces in accordance with his own policy. But, as soon as the ruler happened to be a weakling and the power at the centre waned, or when the trusted nobles and courtiers conspired against the emperor, the provincial governors naturally took advantage of the slackness of supervision and seized the reins of administration in their own hands.

After the all-powerful rule of Alla-ud-din Khilji and the predominating power of Muhammad Tughlaq, succeeded by the able administration of Firoze, there was a reaction once more. The later Tughlaqs, the Sayyids, and the Lodis had none of the talents and governing abilities of their predecessors who carved out the Muhammadan empire in India. Naturally it gave an opportunity to the provincial governors to declare their independence and get out of the control of the so-called Delhi emperors, who were by now mere puppets in the hands of intriguing nobles and selfish and ambitious courtiers. Taimur's attack in 1398 was a death-blow to the imperial power of the rulers at Delhi.

All these factors led to complete anarchy at the centre and the establishment and consolidation of independent kingdoms in various parts of India, such as Kashmir, Bengal, Malwa, Jaunpur, Khandesh, Gujarat, Gulbarga, etc. All those sultans issued their own coins for about two to three centuries until their kingdoms were once more absorbed in the Mughal empire under Akbar and his successors. Thus, from the numismatic point of view, the history of various provinces and the study of their coinage form a very vast subject for research. A good deal of spade work is already done by pioneer numismatists in almost all the branches of this period. But, as we go deeper and investigate, we find that there is still so much to be done in each of them. We have therefore taken upon ourselves to bring to light a large number of new types of coins of the sultans of Gujarat unnoticed and unpublished hitherto. Fortunately the cabinet of this museum has a very rich collection to afford us with greater facility to issue a publication exclusively of coins of this dynasty of Gujarat.

Should the scholars of every province or the authorities of the various provincial museums be able to concentrate upon the collection of coins of local interest and issue exclusive publications of this nature, a flood of light will be thrown on the vast field of numismatics that still stands unexplored before us.

HISTORICAL OUTLINE.

It is neither necessary nor appropriate for the purposes of introducing the subject-matter of this catalogue to our readers to narrate a detailed history of the sultans of Gujarat in these pages. What we are concerned with is only an outline of the history of those rulers with special reference to coins. It is therefore proposed to deal with only such of the incidents, circumstances, and historical events during the regimes of those sultans as are essential for following the growth, development, and decay of the coinage of the dynasty. Those who are interested in details may refer to historical works such as (1) *Tarikh-i-Ferishta*, by Muhammad Qasim, surnamed *Ferishta ;* (2) *Mirat-i-Sikandari,* by Sikandar bin Muhammad ; (3) *Mirat-i-Ahmadi*, by Ali Muhammad Khan; and (4) the *Bombay Gazetteer*, vol. I, part I, by Colonel J. W. Watson.

In the year A.D. 1391, during the reign of Nasir-al-din Muhammad Shah IV Tughlaq on the throne of Delhi as emperor of India, Zafar Khan, one of his nobles and a distant relative, was appointed viceroy of Gujarat and sent to chastise Farhut-al-Mulk Rasti Khan, who had rebelled with the idea of becoming independent of the paramount power at Delhi. At Kambhu, in the district of Anhilwad Pattan, Rasti Khan was defeated and slain and Zafar Khan founded on the site of the battle the town of Jitpur.

At Delhi Muhammad IV died in 1392; and, as his son Sikandar, also, met the same fate after hardly ruling for a month and a half, his second son, Nasir-ud-din Mahmud II, was proclaimed emperor. Some of the nobles wanted Sikandar's son to succeed his father. In the midst of this unsettled state of affairs Taimur invaded India in the year A.D. 1398, and towns through which he passed, and Delhi, the capital, were subjected to horrible massacre and plunder. Mahmud II fled for safety, and, after some wandering, ultimately approached Zafar Khan at the gates of Pattan. But, as Zafar Khan did not help him to march to Delhi, he got disgusted and went to Malwa. There he heard about Nusrat being turned out by his vazir, Iqbal Khan, and he therefore returned to Delhi in A.D. 1402. It was a difficult task for him to keep in control the various provincial governors who, taking advantage of his incapacity, started carving out independent kingdoms for themselves.

Tatar Khan was detained at Delhi when Zafar Khan was sent to Gujarat, but in the confusion that followed the death of Sultan Muhammad IV he escaped from Delhi and conspired for the imperial throne. Having failed in his attempts, he fled to Gujarat with the idea of getting support from his father, who was too shrewd to be involved in that fruitless attempt.

Tatar Khan, however, became restive and, having imprisoned his father, ascended the throne with the title Nasir-ud-duniya wa-ud-din Muhammad Shah.

Zafar secretly sought the help of his brother, Shams Khan, who poisoned the hot-headed Tatar while he was on his way to conquer Delhi. Zafar Khan got back his liberty and the governorship. Full of remorse, he was loath to continue, and declared Ahmad Khan, his grandson, as his successor. He, however, could not wait till the natural death of his grandfather, and, under the pretext of punishing him for the murder of his father, forced him to drink a cup of poison.

After the death of his grandfather Ahmad ascended the throne with the title of Nasir-ud-duniya wa-ud-din Abul-fath Ahmad Shah. He became the virtual founder of the dynasty, and during the course of 33 years' rule (A.H.) 813-846 extended his power far and wide by leading expeditions against Junagadh, Champaner, Idar, and Malwa.

Ahmad, in the year A.H. 813, began to build on the banks of the Sabarmati near the village named Asawal, the present city of Ahmedabad, and styled it Shahr-i-Mu'azzam—the great city. He added to the beauty of the city by erecting several public buildings which are even to-day considered as among the best specimens of Gujarat architecture. With the idea of keeping in check the Chief of Idar, who, when attacked, was retiring into the hills near by, Ahmad built the fort which he styled Ahmadnagar about eighteen miles south-west of Idar and on the banks of the Hathimati river. The date of building this city can be ascertained to be A.H. 829 on the strength of a coin of that date from this mint.

Muhammad II (*A.H. 846-855*). Muhammad Shah II succeeded his father, who died in 846. He was weak and merciful to a fault, and the period of his rule, extending over nine years is, more or less, uneventful. When Mahmud Khalji of Malwa invaded Gujarat with a large army, he, instead of fighting, took to flight like a coward. Naturally, the officers got disgusted with him and had him poisoned through one of his own relatives.

Ahmad Shah II (*A.H. 855-863*).—Jalal Khan, his son and successor, ascended the throne with the title of Qutb-ud-duniya wa-ud-din ("The Polestar of the World and of the Faith") Ahmad Shah. He met Mahmud Khalji at Kapadvanja and gave him a crushing defeat. He also made several unsuccessful attempts at capturing Chitor; and ultimately, when he led an expedition accompanied by the Sultan of Malwa, the Rana promised to pay the tribute. It is doubtful whether he died from a sword wound or from the effect of poison administered by his queen.

Daud Shah.—Qutb-ud-din was succeeded by his uncle, Daud Shah. On ascending the throne, however, he, by giving a high office to a low-born man and by other foolish acts, lost the confidence of his nobles, who dethroned him and placed Mahmud Shah, son of Ahmad Shah, on the throne of Gujarat.

Mahmud I (*Begda*) (*A.H. 863-977*).—Mahmud Shah Begda was the greatest of all Gujarat sultans, and during his reign the prosperity of the kingdom reached its highest zenith. His coinage was equally rich in variety and workmanship, and his coins, known as Mahmudis, can be presented as the best specimens of caligraphy. His military operations and his skill in civil administration are simply superb. Like Ahmad I, he founded two towns, namely, Mustafabad and Muhammadabad, and established mints at both places. He twice attacked Raja Mandlik of Girnar, once in A.H. 871 and again in 874. In the second attempt, when the fort of Girnar was besieged, a good deal of resistance was offered by Mandlik, but ultimately, for want of provisions, he had to surrender the fort and embrace Islam. Mahmud built a city on the site and called it Mustafabad.

Raval Jaysingh of Champaner attacked and killed one of Mahmud's generals, and Mahmud went in person to punish the raja for his impudence. After a protracted siege for a year or so the raja performed johar and sallied forth for a free fight. He was captured; but, unlike Raja Mandlik, he refused to embrace Islam, and paid the penalty by suffering death. This Champaner was given a new name, Muhammadabad, and both names occur side by side as the full title of the mint town on the coins issued from this place.

Muzaffar II (A.H. 917-932).—Mahmud's son, Khalil Khan, succeeded him and adopted the title of Muzaffar II. He was pious, learned, and merciful, and was styled Muzaffar the Clement. He lacked the sternness required for a ruler of those times, and the result was that he was involved in repeated disturbances in Malwa and had to fight for the greater period of his reign with the Ranas of Chitor and Idar. In his old age he grew more and more religious and often offered his life for the welfare of his people.

Sikandar (A.H. 932).—Muzaffar's eldest son, Sikandar, succeeded his father, but he incurred the displeasure of old ministers by bestowing favours on his inexperienced young friends. In his attempt to dispose of Imad-ul-mulk, one of the trusted followers of his father, he was forestalled by the other party and, prematurely murdered.

Mahmud Shah II (A.H. 932-933).—Imad-ul-mulk proclaimed Sikandar's brother, Nasir Khan, a child of six years, as sultan, with the title Mahmud Shah II. The other nobles could not tolerate this high-handedness of Imad-ul-mulk, and they invited Bahadur Khan, the second son of Muzaffar II, who was on his way to Jaunpur, to claim and fight for the throne. He readily agreed, proceeded to the capital, got rid of Imad-ul-mulk, as also Mahmud II, and ascended the throne in the year A.H. 932.

Bahadur Shah (A.H. 933-943).—The whole period of Bahadur's reign was one of continuous warfare. True to his name, he, like a brave (Bahadur) soldier, led expeditions against the kings of Khandesh, Berar, Malwa, and Chitor, and, even before he had settled terms with the Rana of Chitor, the Mughal Emperor Humayun, whom he had offended by not surrendering Muhammad Zaman Mirza, the grandson of a daughter of the Emperor Babar, marched against him and inflicted several crushing defeats on him. He fled to Mandu, Champaner, and Cambay one after the other, being hotly pursued by the conqueror. Ultimately he had to seek shelter from the Portuguese at Div. At this juncture Humayun had to return hurriedly as Sher Shah, the Governor of Bengal, had revolted. Bahadur again gathered his forces and completely routed the army left by Humayun and regained his lost possessions. But Bahadur was destined for disturbances and he had to march against the Portuguese who, instead of building a factory, as permitted by Bahadur in consideration of the shelter given to him, constructed a fort at Div. Bahadur was invited by the Portuguese governor for a compromise, and was treacherously murdered while returning.

Muhammad III.—Muhammad Farukhi of Khandesh, son of Bahadur's sister, was invited to the throne; but, knowing the fate of his maternal uncle, he passed his time in prayer and fasting, and succeeded in courting death after a month or so.

Mahmud III (A.H. 943-961).—Mahmud III, Bahadur's nephew, son of his brother, Latif Khan, was thereafter placed on the throne by the nobles at the tender age of eleven. Naturally, he was a king only in name, while Darya Khan, one of his ministers, was all-powerful. In course of time Mahmud became restless, and, being unable to submit to the restraint, desired to throw off his yoke. Darya Khan thereupon placed another boy on the throne with the title of Muzaffar III, and caused coins to be struck in his name. Mahmud, however, was successful in maintaining his hold as he was popular with his subjects. He, however, could not agree with Darya Khan's life of pleasure and sensuality and fled to Dhandhuka on being invited by Alam Khan Lodi with the promise of making him independent of Darya Khan. Darya Khan's followers also deserted him and he was captured and confined in the fort of Surat.

Burhan, a boy of mean origin, attracted the attention of Mahmud, who appointed him against the wishes of his nobles as a Shoe-Bearer. He gathered strength, and in course of time aspired to the throne. With this end in view he one night offered Mahmud a cup of poisoned sharbat and stabbed him with a dagger. The next day he got all the nobles slaughtered at the hands of a few of the army of Baghmars, or tiger-slayers. He sat on the throne, and, dressed in royal garments, started in procession through the city. Shirwan Khan, one of the surviving nobles, knew of this; and having met him on the way, with one blow cut him into two.

Ahmad III (A.H. 961-968).—Etimad Khan, one of the Amirs who was in charge of the harem, and who had secured the confidence of the late sultan, was consulted as to the possibility of a prince being born in the near future. He replied in the negative, but advised the nobles about a distant relative living at Ahmedabad. The boy was immediately sent for and placed on the throne, with the title of Ahmad Shah III. Other nobles, headed by Ikhtiyar-ul-mulk, tried to put forward Shahu as claimant to the throne, but they were defeated near Mahmudabad and forced to disperse. Internal dissensions hastened the downfall of the Sultanat. Mubarak Shah of Khandesh, who invaded Gujarat, was bribed with the surrender of Sultanpur and Nandarbar. Some other nobles called in the Portuguese for help in retaining Surat and agreed to part with Daman and Sanjan. Ahmad got disgusted with Etimad Khan and yearned for independence, but the latter was too quick; and the sultan's dead body was found one morning on the sands of the Sabarmati.

Muzaffar III (*A.H. 968-980*).—Etimad Khan, the Kingmaker, was again approached by the nobles, and he produced a child named Nathu or Habib and represented on oath that he was the child of Sultan Mahmud. The boy of twelve was thus accepted as king, with the title of Muzaffar III. Signs of the downfall of the Sultanat were too evident, and Muzaffar's reign of about twelve years was the period in which several powerful nobles and neighbours were fighting among themselves to carve out appropriate and convenient portions of territory for themselves. Etimad Khan ultimately invited the Mughal Emperor Akbar to invade and annex Gujarat to his dominions. Sultan Muzaffar was secured and made a prisoner. Coins were ordered to be struck and the Khutba to be read in the name of Akbar Padshah. During succeeding years Akbar had to return now and again to crush new aspirants to the Gujarat throne which was far off from the Mughal capital at Agra.

Muzaffar was taken by Akbar with him to Agra and was given Sarangpur and Ujjain in jagir. His movements, however, created suspicion, and he was imprisoned by his father-in-law, Munim Khan Khanan. In 991 he managed to escape and come to Gujarat. He was tempted by some disaffected nobles to try once more for the throne. The idea appealed to him, and, gathering an army, he marched to Ahmedabad, and, with the help of local nobles, he succeeded, and again sat on the throne after eleven years and issued coins in his name from the Ahmadabad mint. When the emperor knew of this, he sent Rahim Khan as the new viceroy with instructions to drive out Muzaffar and take possession of Gujarat. Muzaffar offered strong resistance, but was defeated and forced to fly to Mahmudabad and thence to Cambay. He was treacherously surrendered to the Mughal viceroy by King Bharmal I of Cutch. Muzaffar was too shrewd to remain a captive in the hands of the Mughal viceroy, and at the earliest opportunity he killed himself by cutting his throat with a razor. Uneasy lies the head that wears a crown!

COINAGE AND COIN TYPES.

A study of human psychology reveals that one is loath to welcome sudden alterations in the matter of favourite articles of daily use. He is all the more careful in recognizing a currency which he is not used to or familiar with. That is perhaps the reason why even the bravest and most furious conquerors or the most powerful monarchs could not affect an abrupt change in the currency of the land which they could, by virtue of their sword or otherwise, acquire in the twinkling of an eye. The political conquest has therefore been no indication of an innovation or triumph in the numismatic field.

The history of numismatics has, on this account, been a natural criterion of the degree of recognition or popularity of a ruler not only with the financers and bankers, but with the ordinary masses. The rulers were therefore bound to design their issues on the lines of the current coinage and effect the necessary changes in type, shape, and size bit by bit so that the evolution of coinage is as if it were a gradual and natural sequence of the passage of time and familiarity of the ruling race.

From this point of view, if we examine the coinage from the earliest times, we would be able to find an almost unbroken link between our times and the remotest past so far as numismatics is concerned.

The coinage of Gujarat was accordingly an adaptation of issues from the coinage of the Tughlaqs, whose power was supreme in Gujarat, and whose coinage was recognized throughout the land before Zafar Khan declared his independence of the imperial authority and sat on the throne of Gujarat as the founder of the glorious Gujarat sultanant with the title of Muzaffar I. Then, during the rule of his successors also, we find a marked and gradual shifting from one type of coin to the other in accordance with the circumstances and needs from time to time.

(*Muzaffar I*, *A.H. 810-813*).—Let us at the outset examine the coinage of Muzaffar I and see how far it was akin to those of his predecessors. Unfortunately, as no gold or silver coins of this ruler are hitherto known, we are at a loss to say anything about them. His copper coins resemble in shape and size the copper issues of Mahmud Shah II Tughlaq. They have the name of the sultan on the reverse, and his title Shams-ud-duniya wa-ud-din on the obverse. Out of the two known copper ones one has the date A.H. 813 clear enough on the obverse. While the descriptive portion of the coins in this catalogue was already printed, my friend, Pandit R. L. Antani of Udaipur, showed me a coin of this ruler that he recently secured. It bears the date 810—the very first year of his reign.

Ahmad I (*A.H. 813-846*).—His gold coins have not been noticed so far, and in silver also only five* pedigree coins are known, one of which is in the Prince of

* (*i*) No. 307 of Thomas, with date A.H. 828 in figures.
(*ii*) No. 3 in this catalogue, with date 835 ; N.S. XXVI, 1915, Taylor.
(*iii*) Cabinet of B.B.R.A.S.; date is illegible; N.S. VI., 1905, Taylor.
(*iv*) American N.S. of New York; date 830 or 840.
(*v*) British Museum, London; date 844 ; N. Ch. (5th Series), volume IV, page 103.

Wales's Museum Cabinet (No. 3). They are dated A.H. 828, 830, 835, and 844, and weigh from 166 to 173 grains. The legend seems to have been copied from the gold and silver coins of Mahmud II Tughlaq. They have on the obverse the legend As-sultan al-a'zam Nasir-ud-duniya wad-din Abul-Fateh and on the reverse the legend in square reads Ahmad Shah bin Muhammad Shah bin Muzaffar Shah Khuld Khilafatahu, giving the names of Ahmad I, Muhammad I, and Muzaffar I; and the date, not in numerals, but in Arabic characters, runs on all the four margins after the fashion of the Delhi sultans.

Copper—

Type No. 1.—Early thick and dumpy coins without mint and date. The earlier copper coins (Nos. 4-29) are similar to those of Muzaffar I, with some additions and alterations. They have thus the name of the Sultan Ahmad on the reverse, and the title Nasir-ud-duniya wad-din on the obverse. Coins numbered 4 to 7 have the quatrefoil and the circle over "he" of Ahmad, while Nos. 8-15 have only the circle on them; No. 8 has on it the letters As-sultan al-a'zam on the obverse in place of the usual epithet Nasir....Nos. 22 and 23 are thin pieces, with some difference in caligraphy; Nos. 28 and 29 have additional letters Abul Fateh on the obverse; Nos. 15 and 21 to 27 are quarter pieces weighing from 35 to 30 grains.

Type No. 2.—Thin pieces, Ahmadnagar mint. The remaining coins, Nos. 30-101 are all of; Ahmadnagar mint. Both the varieties have on the obverse the title Nasir-ud-duniya wad-din with the date in the lower half, but the second variety has the additional words As-sultan al-a'zam towards the top border. There is no difference in the reverse legend of both the varieties, and they bear the name of the Sultan Ahmad Shah in a square, and the name of the mint, Shahr-i-Humayun, Ahmadnagar, running over all the four margins. A large number of coins seems to have been issued from this mint almost every year from A.H. 829 to 846. Coin dated A.H. 834 is not noticed so far; coin No. 74 has a slightly different caligraphy, and Alif of Ahmad is omitted perhaps through an oversight; No. 75 is dated A.H. 827, *i.e.*, two years earlier than the accepted date A.H. 829 for the opening of the Ahmadnagar mint. Whole pieces vary in weight between 148 and 111 grains; half pieces between 73 and 56 grains; and quarter pieces between 30 and 42 grains.

Muhammad II (*A.H. 846-855*).—The coins of Muhammad II can be divided into three main types.

1st Type, Nos. 102-104.—These coins have the legend As-sultan al-a'zam Ghiyasud-duniya wad-din on the obverse, and Abul Muhamid Muhamud Shah as-sultan and date on the reverse. The last of these is a half-size coin weighing 66 grains.

2nd Type, Nos. 105-117.—It is difficult to trace the origin of the real cause of the issue of the rare, beautiful, and extra heavy coins with the legend in the couplet form. *Mirat-i-Sikandari* mentions that Muhammad's father, Ahmad, "had a poetical bent of mind, and some of his verses in praise of Saint Sayyid Burhan-ud-din are extant." It is not unlikely that the son may have inherited this poetical genius from his father, and his life of pleasure and luxury might have increased his love for poetry. The couplet runs over both sides of the coin and reads thus :

Obverse.—Sikka-i-Sultan Ghiyas-ud-din Muhammad Shah bad (here comes the date).

Reverse.—Tabadaruzzarb-i-gardun qurs-i-meher-o-mah bad.

The couplet may be translated as follows :—

May the coin of Sultan Muhammad Shah, the Aid of the Faith, remain

So long as in the mint of heaven the discs of the sun and the moon remain.

These couplet coins are broader in size, measuring, on an average, ·9 inches and heavier in weight weighing from, 195 to 220 grains.

3rd Type Nos. 118-127.—These coins are more or less of the same type, though there is some difference in the arrangement of the legend :

Obverse.—Ghiyas-ud-duniya waud-din.

Reverse.—Muhammad Shah As-sultan and date.

The first four have As-sultan inscribed above and Muhammad Shah below while in the rest the order is reversed.

Ahmad II (A.H. 855-863).—A unique silver pedigree coin similar to those issued by Ahmad I is acquired for the British Museum. Unfortunately, the date is not quite legible, though some traces can, on minute examination, be seen on the coin. The legend on it can be read as follows :

Obverse.—As-sultan al-a'zam Qutb-ud-duniya waud-din Abul-Muzaffar—traces of date.

Reverse.—Ahmad Shah bin Muhammad Shah bin Ahmad Shah bin Muhammad Shah bin Muzaffar Shah Khuld Khilafatahu.

It weighs 174 grains and is one inch in diameter.

2nd Type, Nos. 128-143.—The second type is the one commonly met with in copper. It has the legend Qutb-ud-duniya wad-din Abul Muzaffar on the obverse, and Ahmad Shah As-sultan and date on the reverse. Over and above the three ordinary denominations three heavier pieces of 216, 209, and 186 grains, similar to the couplet pieces of the previous ruler, are also known.

3rd Type, Nos. 144-149.—For the first time in Ahmad II's rule billon coins were minted for Gujarat. These have close affinity with similar coins of Alam Shah (A.H. 849-855) and Bahlol Lodi (A.H. 855-894) ruling at Delhi. The reason of his adopting this title is given by Mr. A. Master in *Numismatic Supplement* No. XL, page 7. He writes, "His laqab Qutb has an obvious connection with Qutb-ul-aqtab, the holy Bukhara Sayyid, the patron of Vajih-ul-mulk. The history of Qutb-ud-din shows that, until his quarrel with Shah Alam, which ended in his death, the sultan was much under the influence of the Bukhara Sayyids. He was the first to adopt the title of Amir-ul-mumnin and Abul-Muzaffar, both of which Altamsh used." The legend reads as follows:

Obverse.—Qutb-ud-duniya waud-din Ahmad Shah As-sultan.

Reverse.—Al-Khalifa Amir-ul-mominin Khuldat Khilafat and date.

Coins Nos. 150 to 152 are very similar to those of the 2nd, type and differ from them inasmuch as the words Abul-Muzaffar are absent on the obverse.

Mahmud I (*A.H. 863-917*)—The only known gold coin of Mahmud I dated A.H. 914, weighing 183·6 grains and measuring ·85 inch, is in the British Museum. The legend on the obverse reads:

Al-wa-siq batāeed-ur-Rahman.

Nasir-ud-duniya waud-din Abul-Fateh.

On the reverse there is the name of the Sultan Mahmud Shah bin Muhammad Shah As-sultan in double square and the date 914 in the bottom margin.

Silver.—

A full size (9·″) pedigree coin weighing 172 grains is in the collection of the Bombay Branch of the Royal Asiatic Society. The date is not clear, but appears to be either 864 or 869. Dr. Taylor's reading of the date as 865 is not correct as 5 in the form of a circle is not to be seen on coins of this period. The lower portion of the unit figure is lost and the circle that is left seems to be the upper portion either of 4 or 9.

The legend on the obverse reads :

Al-wa-siq billa al-minnan Nasir-ud-duniya wa-ud-din Abul-Fateh

and on the reverse there is the genealogy of Mahmud right up to the founder of the dynasty. It reads : Mahmud Shah ibn Muhammad Shah ibn Ahmad Shah ibn Muhammad Shah ibn Muzaffar Shah as-sultan. The date is at the lower bottom.

Ordinary Silver Coins.—

From the time of this sultan the currency is more or less standardized, and the same pattern is continued right up to the end, with few minor differences in weight, size, and the arrangement of the legend, etc.

Mahmud's silver coins were issued in large numbers from the Mustafabad (Junagadh) and Muhammadabad (Champaner) mints. Some issues of the latter mint bear the mint name Shahr-i-mukarram, Muhammadabad, while others have the name Muhammadabad as well as Champaner inscribed on them. There are four coins of the Dib mint three of which are dated A.H. 900.

All these coins have, more or less, the same legend : Nasir-ud-duniya wa-ud-din Abul-Fateh, the date on the obverse, the name of the sultan in the square, and the mint name in the margins on the reverse. There is a number of minor variations in the position of the date and mint, and the arrangement, etc., of the legend which are all detailed in the body of the catalogue, and which need not be narrated here over again.

Mahmud's copper and billon coins, also of the same type, were issued in large numbers, and about 160 have been exhibited in the Museum cabinet. They are all from the same two mints—Mustafabad and Muhammadabad.

Some interesting peculiarities must be mentioned here. Coin No. 258 has on it the additional names of the sultan's brother, Qutb Shah, and his father Muhammad.

No. 269, acquired from Sir Currimbhoy Ebrahim's collection, has on it clearly the date A.H. 862 as against the date A.H. 863 given by all historians as the date of the accession of Mahmud.

No. 303 from Mustafabad, with date 871 (A.D. 1466), clearly proves that coins were minted at the end of his first expedition against the Raja of Junagadh.

Billon coins (Nos. 321-324a) have the dates in Arabic characters running on the margins of the reverse in place of the mint.

The letters "fi" meaning "at" are to be noticed for the first time on coins Nos. 342-349.

Coin No. 408 is the only specimen issued from the Muhammadabad mint. It is abnormal, both in design and weight. It is modelled after the silver variety (No. 244), and weighs 318 grains.

The top margin of No. 409 bears the letters Khittah, which is usually associated with the mint name Dib.

On coin No. 410, over the name of the sultan and his father, there is the mint name at the top of which the initial letter or letters are not legible, and which can therefore be read either as Ahmadabad or Muhammadabad.

Muzaffar II (A.H. 917-932).—

Gold.—

Out of five gold coins of Muzaffar II known so far four are in the British Museum London, and one is in the Indian Museum, Calcutta. Two of them are dated A.H. 920 while the remaining three are dated A.H. 924, 929, and 932 respectively. The weight varies from 176 to 179 grains, and the size from ·75 to ·8 inches. The legend, except for slight variations in the arrangement of the words, is the same on all these coins, and reads as follows :

Obverse.—Al-mueed bataeed ur-Rehman Shams-ud-duniya wa-ud-din Abun-nasr.

Reverse.—Muzaffar Shah bin Mahmud Shah As-sultan and date at the bottom.

Silver.—

The legend on the silver coins is the same as that on the gold ones, but very few of them bear mint names. Two coins in the Phayre Provincial Museum, Rangoon, are issues of the Muhammadabad mint, and are dated A.H. 921 and 923.

Nos. 440-443 are coins on which the mint name was incorrectly read as Khanpur. The name has now been correctly read Fi Burhanpur by Mr. C. R. Singhal.

No. 446, which is a beautiful specimen issued from the Mustafabad mint, has on it the additional phrase Khaldullah Mulkahu to be seen for the first time on the coins of this period.

Copper.—

The copper coin No. 470 dated A.H. 918 has also the phrase Khaldullah Mulkahu. It follows therefore that this was adopted by him soon after his occupying the throne.

From coins Nos. 490a-492a we gather that copper coins were also issued from the Burhanpur mint.

Mahmud II (A.H. 932).—

Mahmud was on the throne for only four months when his brother, Bahadur got rid of him by poisoning him. There are four coins—Nos. 513-516—of Gujarat fabric which bear the name of Nasir Shah as sultan on the reverse and can therefore be safely assigned to this Mahmud II, whose name, while he was a prince, was Nasir Khan. Unfortunately, none of these coins is dated.

Bahadur Shah (A.H. 932-943).—

Silver.—

Bahadur Shah had also the privilege of issuing a pedigree coin dated A.H. 933. The weight and size are 129 grains and ·8 inches respectively. The legend starts with the title Qutb-ud-duniya waud-din Abul-Fazal and ends with the name of Bahadur Shah bin Muzaffar Shah. The rest of the legend on the reverse takes the genealogy right up to Muzaffar I. Few ordinary silver coins that are known are dated A.H. 941 and 943. One with the date 943 is in the British Museum and has on it the additional letters " Al-adal " along with " As-sultan."

Copper.—

Bahadur's copper coins Nos. 526-531 make a type by themselves wherein the legend on the reverse is nothing but the date written in Arabic characters. The letter Sanah is in the centre and the top portion reads Asantin, Salas, or Arba't, as well as Salsin (in crude form), and the bottom reads Tusumayt and the date 932 to 934 in figures as the case may be.

Shah-i-Hind Type.—

Dr. Taylor, in his article in *Numismatic Supplement* No. XXXIII, had, for lack of any better hypothesis, assigned these coins to Babar and Humayun. Eight years after this Professor S. H. Hodivala tackled this problem more successfully, and he suggested, in *Numismatic Supplement* No. XL, that these coins should more appropriately be assigned to Bahadur Shah of Gujarat. This was further strengthened when he discovered the traces of the mint Shahr-i-mukrram, Muhammadabad (Champaner), on the margins of some of them.

These coins bear the followng couplet as the legend running all over the obverse and reverse :

Harkera ru-yo riwaji hast bar sathe zamin
Sikka-i-Iqbal-i-Shah-i-Hind darad bar jabin

This can be translated as.—

Whoever possesses name and fame on the surface of the earth bears on his forehead the stamp of the glory of the sovereign of India.

They were issued, it seems, only for six years from A.H. 935 to 940. Dr. Taylor refers to a coin dated 934, but it is not forthcoming. These six or seven years of Bahadur were full of stirring events and prosperity. He successfully attacked in succession the Deccan kings, the Ruler of Bidar, the Sultan of Malwa, and the Raja of Ujjain and became virtual master of all the southern countries. He had aspiration, even for the throne of Delhi. It is not improbable that he designed this special type of currency to be introduced in those countries as a mark of his triumph. These coins can be separated into two varieties on the strength of the different arrangements of the legend, etc. On the first variety the reverse legend is inscribed in a square, and the name of the mint runs on the four margins of the coin. In coins of the second variety the square is absent, andthe legend is written in lines one over the other. The mint name is not to be seen on them at all. Coins of this second variety seem to have been issued only during A.H. 938 and 939.

Mahmud Shah III (A.H. 943-961).—

Gold.—

Twelve muhars of this sultan are known so far, and they are all of the same type, weight 185 grains, size ·8″, and bear the same legend, *viz.*

Al-wasiq billah al-minnan Nasir-ud-duniya waud-din Abul-Fateh on the obverse and Mahmud Shah bin Latif Shah As-sultan and date on the reverse.

Dates known, so far, are six in number. They are A.H. 946, 947, 949, 950 956, and 960.

Silver.—

The silver coins also bear, more or less, the same legend on the obverse and reverse, but they can be grouped into five separate lots because of the difference in the arrangement of the legend, the position of the date, and such other points of minor importance.

In Nos. 600-606 (*a*) the legend on the obverse has to be read from the top downwards; (*b*) the legend on the reverse is enclosed in a double square with peaked sides ; and (*c*) the date is over Mahmud.

In the next lot (Nos. 607-612) the legend on the obverse runs from the bottom upwards; and the date is given at the bottom.

In the third lot (Nos. 613-618a) the legend on the reverse is inscribed in a scalloped circle, and the date is over Latif.

Nos. 619-625 have the reverse legend in a double square with peaked sides. In the last lot, Nos. 626-629, the date is over " bin; " and in No. 628 the name Ahmad is legible on the bottom margin, which leads us to infer that these coins might have been minted at Ahmadabad.

Copper—.

Copper coins bear a portion of the same legend, but only a few of them have clear mint names on them. Some striking points are noted below :

(*a*) No. 630 has the mint name Muhammadabad, with its epithet clearly inscribed in the four margins on the obverse;

(*b*) No. 658 dated A.H. 950 has on it the name of the sultan in Devanagari characters. Of the four letters the last two, *viz.*, " Moo " and " Da, " are quite legible;

(*c*) No. 659 has the date A.H. 951 inscribed on both sides,

(*d*) Nos. 665a-679 are positively the issues of the Ahmadabad mint, and the name of the mint, with its epithet Shahr-i-Mu'azzam can be clearly read.

(*e*) No. 696a has the word Khittah on the top margin on the reverse which is associated with the mint name Dib;

(*f*) Nos. 704 and 705 are issues of the Daulatabad-Baroda mint. On the former Daulatabad is quite clear, and traces of the first two letters of Baroda can also be traced, but with difficulty. On the latter the mint name is too fragmentary to be read ; and

(*g*) On Nos. 708 and 709 one of the Malwa mint marks is given on the obverse.

Ahmad III (*A.H. 961-968*).—

The gold coin of Ahmad III was not known till 1925-26 when the Provincial Museum, Lucknow, acquired a beautiful half-muhar weighing 91·5 grains, measuring ·6 inches, and dated A.H. 962. The legend on the coins of all metals is practically the same ; it is seen in full on the silver coin and in fragmentary condition on the gold and copper coins. The full legend reads :

Al motasim billah Ur-rahman Ghiyas-ud-duniya wa-ud-din Abul-Mahamid on the obverse and the reverse gives the name of the Sultan Ahmad Shah, with his father's name, Mahmud Shah, and the date.

The following peculiarities have, however, to be noted :

(*a*) On No. 732a the word " bin " can be read, but the name of the sultan's father, Mahmud, is missing.

(*b*) Nos. 786-794 are issues of the Ahmadabad mint as can be ascertained by fragmentary traces of the name and epithet of the mint.

Muzaffar III (A.H. 968-980 and A.H. 991-992).

Gold.—

Only two coins dated A.H. 970 and 977 are known. They are similar to the coins of Muzaffar II, and the legend is also the same on the obverse. On the reverse the names of the sultan and his father, as well as the dates, are given in a double square.

Silver.—

On the silver coins the legend is the same as on the gold ones, differing only in arrangement, etc. The following special features may be noted :

(*a*) The reverse legend on coins Nos. 797-798 is in a square, while it is in a scalloped circle in coins Nos. 799-803 ;

(*b*) On coins Nos. 804-816 the reverse legend is inscribed in a peaked area, and the name of the father of the sultan is omitted ; and

(*c*) Coin No. 817 dated A.H. 991 is interesting inasmuch as it has on the obverse the Kalima, as is found on the coins of Akbar. On the reverse the date 991 and the mint Ahmadabad can be read over and above the usual names of the sultan and his father.

Copper.—

On the copper coins also the legend is the same, though in fragmentary form. Most of them are of the Ahmadabad mint, as can be gathered from fragments of the mint name or its epithet in the margins.

(*a*) In coin No. 840 there is a Malwa mint mark on the reverse.

(*b*) In coins Nos. 847a-853 we find the couplet, though in a crude form, which is noticed on the reverse of the coins of Muhammad II.

(*c*) On the reverse of No. 859 the mint name Champaner can be read.

(*d*) The obverse side legend on coins Nos. 865 and 889 is the same as is found on the coins of Ahmad III.

MINT TOWNS.

Till recently, only four mint towns of the Gujarat Sultanat were known to numismatists. One more, *viz.*, Khanpur, was tentatively read by Mr. H. N. Wright on a coin sent to him by Dr. Taylor. With the help of several other specimens of the same mint this Khanpur has now been positively read as Burhanpur. Two new mints have come to light as a result of our examination of the coins in this museum. They are Dib and Daulatabad.

1. Ahmedabad : احمدآباد , founded A.H.= 813 or 815 or 816
A.D. 1410 or 1412 or 1413

Epithets : a. شهر معظم Shahr-i-Mu'azzam, the great city.

b. دارالضرب Dar-al-Zarb, the seat of the mint.

(*a*) No silver coin with the mint name Ahmadabad was known so far, though Professor Hodivala has described one with the epithet Shahr-i-Mu'azzam. But the bottom margin of the silver coin in catalogue No. 628 bears Ahmadabad as the name of the mint.

In copper only three coins of Muzaffar III were brought to light, but in our cabinet there are ten dated coins of Mahmud III and four of Ahmad III having this epithet clearly on them.

(*b*) There are one silver and two copper coins in the museum collection which bear the second epithet of this mint, *i.e.*, Dar-al-Zarb. These coins were struck during the second reign of Muzaffar III.

On the top of the reverse of copper coin No. 410 of Mahmud I, dated H (9) 10 'حمدآباد' can be clearly read. Whether this coin was also struck at Ahmadabad or at Muhammadabad is a debatable point.

2. Ahmednagar (now Himmatnagar, in Idar State) احمد نگر founded H 829 or 830=A.D. 1425 or 1426.

Epithet : شهر همایون Shahr-i-Humayun, the auspicious city.

The epithet of this mint, which was doubtfully read by Dr. Taylor as شهر مهانور, the city of great light, was correctly deciphered by Mr. H. N. Wright as شهر همایون the auspicious city. In this collection there are several coins on which the word 'همایون' can be read with certainty.

This mint was uttering copper coins from the year of its founding (H 829, to the year of Sultan Ahmad's death in H 846 except, the year H 834. Coin No. 75 of this mint is dated as early as H 827; it is not known whether this date is a freak, or that the city was founded, and the mint established, earlier than H 829.

It appears that this mint was uttering only coppers, and was exclusively used by Sultan Ahmad. The coins of none of the other sultans nor of any other metal are known to have been struck at this mint.

3. Mustafabad (Girnar or Junagadh) مصطفی باد, founded H 877=A.D. 1472.

Epithet : شہر اعظم Shahr-i-A'zam, the great city.

Dr. Taylor had noticed only three silver issues of this mint of Mahmud I, but in this collection there are twenty-six silver and five billon coins with dates of Mahmud I and two silver coins of Muzaffar II, out of which one is dated H 926. This shows that the mint was functioning till H 926.

In copper the number of coins is fairly large, and they bear dates from H 871 to 912, with few gaps here and there. Coin No. 303 dated 871 marks the first attack against Girnar, though the fort was finally captured in the year H 877. With the exception of this solitary piece which is dated A 871, the rest of the coins bear dates after the year H 877.

4. (*a*) *Muhammad abad* محمد آباد founded H 889=A.D. 1484.

(*b*) *Muhammadabad* alias *Champaner* محمد آباد عرف چانپانیر.

Epithet : شہر مکرم Shahr-i-Mukkaram, the illustrious city.

(*a*) Just as the Ahmadnagar mint was meant only for copper issues, this mint was active mostly with white metal. Dr. Taylor had about thirteen silver coin of this mint, but he had not secured a single copper piece. He therefore believed that the coins were struck there by none except Mahmud I and that too durings the period between H 895 and 904; and that the whole period during which the mint was working does not cover more than twenty-five years. A glance at the *Index of Mints* will, however, show that the coins were struck at this mint not only by Mahmud I, but also by his successors, Muzaffar II, Bahadur Shah, and Mahmud III. The dates found on them are from H 891 to 912, H 921 and 923, H 935 to 940, and H 944 respectively. Copper coins, though their number is very limited, were struck by all the sultans mentioned above, except Muzaffar II. Copper coin No. 410 dated 910 of Mahmud I which bears 'محمد آباد' on the reverse top margin might have probably been issued from this mint.

(*b*) The city's remarkable prosperity can be realised from coins issued from it which bear the mint name محمد آباد عرف چانپانیر. The number of these coins is extremely limited, and in this collection there are only five silvers which belong to Mahmud I. In the legend on the reverse of copper coin No. 859 dated H 977 of Muzaffar III " Zarb Champaner " can be read.

5. *Dib :* خطۂ دیب

All the four coins of this mint—three of silver and one of copper—have been found in Dr. Taylor's collection. Coin No. 254 is figured in his article as No. 32 on plate III, but the mint name seems to have escaped his notice. The date on all the three silver coins is A.H. 900, while on the copper one the date is missing.

6. *Burhanpur* : برهانپور

The mint name on these coins was read by Dr. Taylor as ضربت خانپور, Zarbat Khanpur, but, on more careful examination, it appears that it is ز بر برهانپور, *i.e.*, at Burhanpur.

Four silver, and about the same number of copper, coins issued from the Burhanpur mint by Muzaffar II have come to light. It appears, the mint must have been working for a limited time as the dates found on coins are from H 920 to 923 and 926.

It is inexplicable, so far, why only five coins of Mahmud I issued from this mint in the year A.H. 900 have been obtained, even though Dib was all along in the possession of the Gujarat sultans ever since Zafar Khan secured it in A.H. 804 till the time it was taken over by the Portuguese in A.H. 943 after the death of Bahadur Shah. The existence of one copper of Mahmud III confirms the statement in the *Imperial Gazetteer*, volume XI, page 364, that the after the death of Bahadur Shah Mahmud III twice made attempts to recapture Dib from the Portuguese, but without success. This coin, however, can make us believe that Mahmud III ought to have been successful at least once and held Dib for some time which enabled him to issue coins in his own name from this mint.

On two copper coins of Mahmud I and Mahmud III the legend in the top and left margins respectively can be read as Khittah, which is the attribute preceding Dib, though the actual name of the mint is missing.

7. *Daulatabad.*

In the margin of a solitary copper coin of Mahmud III Daulatabad can be read, though with some doubt. In *Mirat-Ahmadi* it is found that Baroda was also called Daulatabad. This dateless piece might have been struck at Baroda by one of the governors of Sultan Mahmud III.

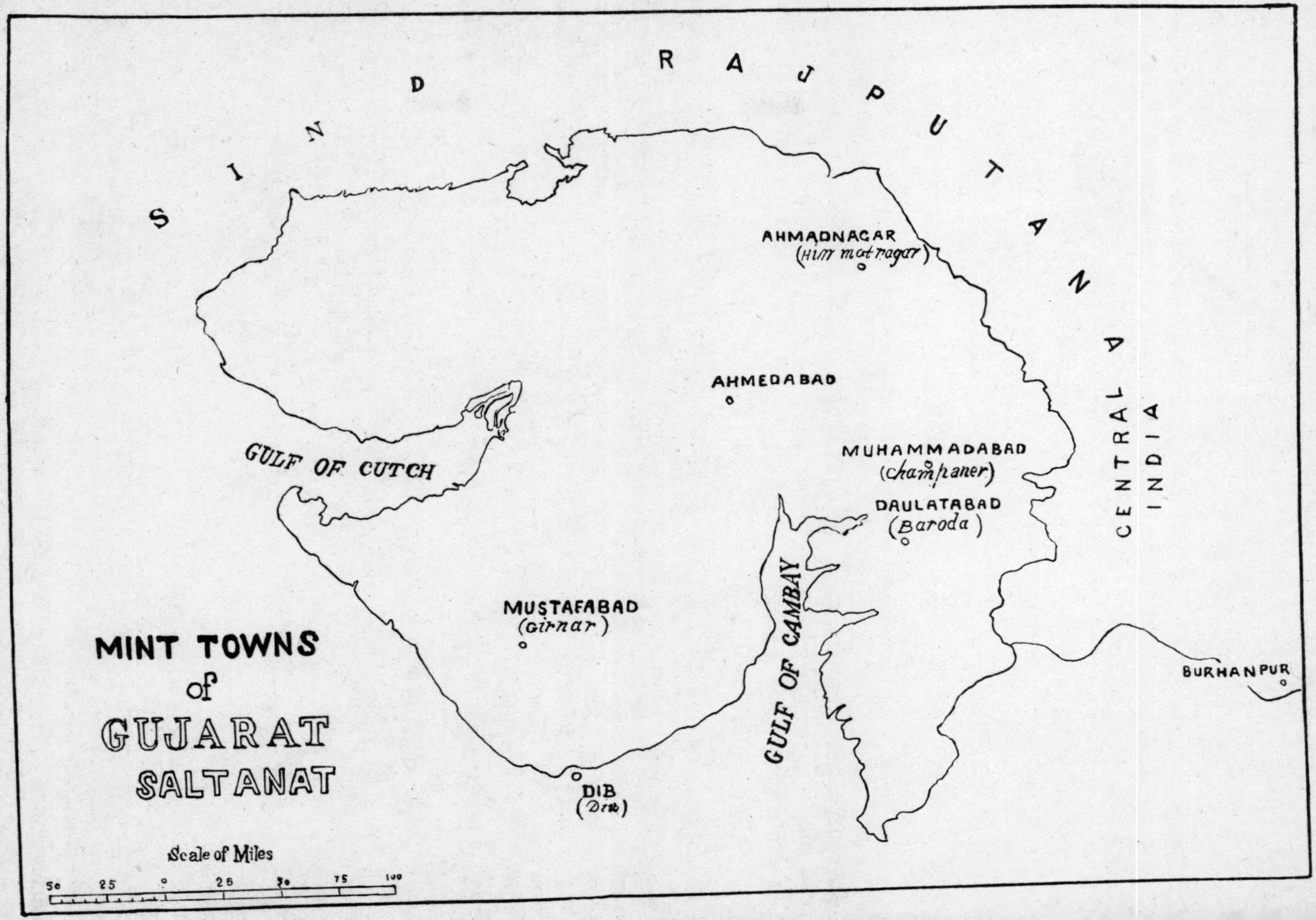
MINT TOWNS
of
GUJARAT
SALTANAT
SIND
RAJPUTANA
CENTRAL INDIA
GULF OF CUTCH
GULF OF CAMBAY
AHMADNAGAR
(Himmatnagar)
AHMEDABAD
MUHAMMADABAD
(Champaner)
DAULATABAD
(Baroda)
MUSTAFABAD
(Girnar)
DIB
(Diu)
BURHANPUR
Scale of Miles
50 25 0 25 50 75 100

WEIGHTS AND STANDARDS.

The metrology of the coins issued by the sultans of Gujarat has hitherto been a tough problem to be solved by the numismatists. In spite of a large number of pecimens being available, the variety of weights is too copious to yield a decisive conclusion in the matter. As early as A.D. 1902 Dr. Taylor contributed a chapter on the weights and measures of these coins and summarised the results of his investigations in two tables showing the various denominations that could be ascertained. Taking a unit of 4 ratis, or 7·4 grains, he postulated ten denominations in silver and ten in copper. *According to him, a "rati" weighed 1·85 grains, and 96 such ratis went for a tola; this made a tola equivalent to 177·6 grains.

In 1908, when Mr. H. N. Wright submitted his contribution in volume II of the *Indian Museum Catalogue*, he held that a rati weighed 1·8 grains only, and 100 such ratis made a tola; this brought a tola to 180 grains. About the denominations he is silent, and evidently agreed with the decision arrived at by Dr. Taylor.

The latest on the subject is a scholarly article from the pen of Professor S. H. Hodivala which appeared in volume II (New Series) of the *Journal of the Bombay Branch of the Royal Asiatic Society* in 1926. In this article he discussed the matter at great length, but could not arrive at any definite conclusions in spite of the very rich collection of coins that he had in his possession. The very copiousness of details, he observed, creates confusion and embarrassment, more so because there is the absence of any literary evidence on the subject, and because the coins themselves, having suffered in weight, due to constant use, cannot give the correct or exact weights for guidance. All the same, he added two fresh denominations in the silver, and six more in the copper,† issues of this series. As regards the difference of opinion in respect of the number of ratis contained in a tola, he thought it hazardous to decide, especially when the difference between the two theories of a tola came only to 2·4 grains; and it became still less in case of halves and quarters.

When we examine these theories in the light of the material at our disposal, it appears that Dr. Taylor was correct in accepting the 96 rati standard for a tola; and it appears that Mr. H. N. Wright also has since revised his theory of 100 ratis (*vide* his joint article in the *Numismatic Supplement*, No. XXXVIII, "On the Metrology of the Early Sultans of Delhi," published in 1924). As has been pointed out, the Gujarat sultans followed closely the style of their contemporaries at Delhi so far as the size, type, and general tone of the legends were concerned. There is no wonder if they had the same standard of weight—*viz.*, that of 96 ratis to a tola—as had their contemporaries at Delhi. A survey of the weights of the copper issues of Ahmad I,

* The denominations are 5, 10, 15, 20; 6, 12, 24; and 8, 16, 32 units in silver; and 4, 8; 5, 10, 20, 30, 45; and 6, 12, 24 units in copper.

† The denominations added are: 2½ and 18 units in silver; and 2½, 15, 18, 22, 27, & 36 units in copper.

II, and III, Mahmud I, Bahadur, and Muzaffar III, which are accepted to be of 80 ratis in weight, makes it clear (from their weight of 145 to 147 grains in respect of full, and 73 to 74 grains in case of half, coins) that Dr. Taylor's observation was correct.

As regards the silver coins issued by Muzaffar II, Dr. Taylor held that they had an issue weight of 60 ratis (*i.e.*, 60×1·85=111 grains), while Mr. Wright was of opinion that the maximum weight of the then rupee was 64 ratis (*i.e.*, 64×1·8= 115·2 grains). As Professor Hodivala did not come across any coin of Muzaffar II or those of his son Bahadur weighing more than 111 grains, naturally he sided with Dr. Taylor. In the cabinet of the Prince of Wales' Museum, however, there is a coin of Muzaffar II dated 929 (No. 468) which weights 115 grains. This evidence goes in favour of Mr. Wright's conclusion.

Denominations.

Dr. Taylor had classified the known silver and copper coins in twenty (ten in silver and ten in copper) different denominations. Professor Hodivala has, on the strength of his own collection, added two more subdivisions in silver and six others in copper, making in all 28 denominations. These denominations ought to be a certain multiple of a common unit which, on a careful examination of coins available, was ascertained by Dr. Taylor to be of 7·4 grains, or 4 ratis. It does not seem feasible for so many denominations to have been quite independent of each other; and, as a result of careful classification, we have been able to group them in several series, as shown below. Evidently there were two, three, or more series current in every ruler's time, and they consisted of a full, half, quarter, and eighth of a coin. In some cases, coins with half as much again the value and weight of a full coin also seem to have been issued :—

	A		B
	Units. Grains.		*Units. Grains.*
Whole pieces	20=144–148	Whole pieces	24=177·6–180
Halves	10=72–74	Halves	12=88·8–90
Quarters	5=36–37	Quarters	6=44·4–45
⅛ Pieces	2½=18–18·5		
	C		D
	Unite. Grains.		*Units. Grains.*
Whole pieces	30=222–225	Whole pieces	32=236–237
Halves	15=115–115·2	Halves	16=118–118·5
Quarters	7½=55·5–57·6	Quarters	8=57·6–59·2
		⅛ Pieces	4=28·8–29·6
	E		F
	Units. Grains.		*Units. Grains.*
Whole pieces	36=259·2–266·4	Whole pieces	45=324–333
Halves	18×133·2–135	Halves	22=158·4–162·8

The last two series, E and F, seem to be 1½ pieces and their halves of B and C series respectively. This leaves only a 27-unit piece in copper which cannot be grouped in any of the above series.

MUẒAFFAR SHÁH I.

Æ No.	Mint	Date	Weight and size	Obverse	Reverse
				COPPER	
1	—	813	Wt. 68 S. ·6	شمس الدنيا والدين ٨١٣	مظفر شاه السلطان Pl. I
2	—		"	"	"

AḤMAD SHÁH I.

				SILVER	
AR 2a	—	828	Wt. 172 S. 1.	السلطان الاعظم الدنيا و ناصر الدين ابو الفتح	In circle احمد شاه بن محمد شاه شاه مظفر خلد خلافته ٨٢٨ *Thomas* No. 307.
3		835	Wt. 173 S. 1.	السلطان الاعظم الدنيا والدين ناصر ابو الفتح	In square احمد شاه بن محمد شاه بن مظفر شاه خلدت خلافته *Margins :—* Top في سنه Left خمس و Bottom ثلاثين Right وثمانمائت Pl. I.

AR No.	Mint	Date	Weight and size	Obverse	Reverse
				SILVER	
3a	—	830 or 840	Wt. 172 S. 1.	As on No. 3.	Area as on No. 3. But top margin فى left ,, سنة bottom ,, ثلاثين or اربعين right ,, وثمانمائة *A.N.S.* No. 220.
3b	—	844	Wt. 166 S. 1·2	,,	,, But left margin اربع bottom ,, اربعين *N: C. 5th series Vol. VI.* P. 103.
				COPPER	
Æ 4 5 6	—	—	Wts. 142 136 131 S. ·65	الدنيا ناصر والدين	السلطان شاه احمد With quatrefoil and circle over ح of احمد Pl. I.
7	—	—	Wt. 66 S. ·55	,,	,,
8	—	—	Wt. 138 S. ·6	الاعظم السلطان	,, Without quatrefoil but circle over ح of Ahmad. Pl. I.
9	—	—	Wt. 139 S. ·5 & ·6 Oblong	As on No. 4.	,,

Æ No.	Mint	Date	Weight and size	Obverse	Reverse
				COPPER	
10	—	—	Wt. 137 S. ·65	As on No. 4.	As on No. 4. Without quatrefoil.
11	—	—	Wt. 129 S. ·65	"	As on No. 8.
12	—	—	Wt. 70 S. ·55	"	"
13	—	—	Wt. 66 S. ·55	"	"
14	—	—	Wt. 62 S. ·5	"	"
15	—	—	Wt. 35 S. ·4	"	"
16	—	—	Wt. 145 S. ·6	"	السلطان شاه احمد Pl. I.

Æ No.	Mint	Date	Weight and size	Obverse	Reverse
				COPPER	
17	—	—	Wt. 142 S. ·6	As on No. 4.	As on No. 4, but with neither quatrefoil nor circle.
18	—	—	Wt. 78 S. ·55	"	"
19	—	—	Wt. 69 S. ·5	"	"
20	—	—	Wt. 65 S. ·5	"	"
21	—	—	Wt. 65 S. ·6	"	"
21a	—	(8) 23	Wt. 71·5 S. ·55	الدنيا ناصر والدين ۲۳ (۸)	السلطان شاه ۲۳(۸) احمد A. N. S. No. 1
22	—	843	Wt. 35 S. ·55	As on No. 4, but ۸۴۳	السلطان شاه احمد

Pl. I.

Æ No.	Mint	Date	Weight and size	Obverse	Reverse
					COPPER
23	—	—	Wt. 30 S. ·55	As on No. 4.	السلطان شاه احمـــد Pl. I.
24	—	—	Wt. 33 S. ·45	"	As on No. 17.
25	—	—	Wt. 32 S. ·4	"	شاه احمد Pl. I.
26	—	—	Wt. 33 S. ·4	نا الدنيا صـــر	" Pl. I.
27	—	—	Wt. 34 S. ·45	شاه احمد	ن السلطا Pl. I.
28	—	—	Wt. 137 S. ·7	الدنيا ناصـــر والدين ابو الفتح	As on No. 17.
29	—	—	Wt. 142 S. ·7	الدنيا ناصـــر والدين ابوالفتح	" Pl. I.

Æ No.	Mint	Date	Weight and size	Obverse	Reverse
				COPPER	
30	Ahmad-nagar Shahr-i-Humayun	829	Wt. 67 S. ·7	الدنيا و ناصــــر الدين ٨٢٩	In square السلطان احمد شاه *Margins:—* Top شهر Left همايون Bottom احمد Right نگر Pl. I.
31	(Ahmad) nagar Shahr-i-(Humayun)	830	Wt. 71 S. ·7	,, but ٨٣٠	,, Bottom margin not clear.
32	(Ahmad nagar) Shahr-i-(Humayun)	,,	Wt. 64 S. ·7	,,	,, Margins illegible.
33	Ahmad-nagar	831	Wt. 73 S. ·7	,, but ٨٣١	,, Top and left margins illegible.
34	Ahmad-(nagar) (Shahr-i-) Humayun	,,	Wt. 66 S. ·7	,,	,, Right margin illegible.
35	Ahmad-nagar	,,	Wt. 57 S. ·6	As on No. 33.	As on No. 33.
36	Ahmad-nagar	,,	Wt. 56 S. ·65	,,	,,

Æ No.	Mint	Date	Weight and size	Obverse	Reverse
					COPPER
37	(Ahmad) nagar	831	Wt. 30 S. ·5	As on No. 33.	As on No. 30. Right margin legible.
38	Ahmad-nagar	832	Wt. 68 S. ·65	As on No. 30 but (٨)٣٢	As on No. 33.
39	Ahmad-(nagar)	,,	Wt. 62 S. ·65	,,	As on No. 30. Only bottom margin legible.
40	(Ahmad-nagar) Shahr-i-(Humayun)	833	Wt. 64 S. ·65	As on No. 30 but ٨٣٣	As on No. 32.
41	Ahmad-(nagar) Shahr-i-Humayun	836	Wt. 70 S. ·7	,, but ٨٣٦	As on No. 34.
42	(Ahmad-nagar)	,,	Wt. 65 S. ·7	,,	As on No. 32.
43	(Ahmad-nagar) Shahr-i-Humayun	,,	Wt. 42 S. ·65	,,	As on No. 37.

Æ No.	Mint	Date	Weight and size	Obverse	Reverse
				COPPER	
44	—	836	Wt. 35 S. ·55	As on No. 30.	As on No. 32.
45	Ahmad (nagar) (Shahr-i-) Humayun	837	Wt. 70 S. ·65	,, but (٨)٣٧	As on No. 30. Left and bottom mar-gins legible.
46	(Ahmad nagar)	,,	Wt. 64 S. ·7	,,	As on No. 32.
47	Ahmad-(nagar)	,,	Wt. 35 S. ·55	,,	As on No. 39.
48	Ahmad-nagar	838	Wt. 73 S. ·7	,, but ٨٣٨	As on No. 33.
49	—	,,	Wt. 67 S. ·65	,,	As on No. 32.
50	(Ahmad-nagar) (Shahr-i-) Humayun	,,	Wt. 62 S. ·7	,,	,,

Æ No.	Mint	Date	Weight and size	Obverse	Reverse
				COPPER	
51	—	838	Wt. 33 S. ·5	As on No. 30, but ۸۳۸	As on No. 32.
52	—	839	Wt. 73 S. ·7	,, but (۸)۳۹	,,
53	(Ahmad-nagar)	,,	Wt. 69 S. ·65	,,	As on No. 39.
54	—	,,	Wt. 66 S. ·7	,,	As on No. 32.
55	—	,,	Wt. 34 S. ·55	,,	,,
56	Ahmad-nagar	83x	Wt. 32 S. ·55	As on No. 31.	As on No. 33.
57	Ahmad-(nagar) Shahr-i-Humayun	840	Wt. 70 S. ·65	As on No. 30, but ۸۴۰	As on No. 45.

Æ No.	Mint	Date	Weight and size	Obverse	Reverse
				COPPER	
58	Ahmad-(nagar)	840	Wt. 62 S. ·65	As on No. 30, but ٨٤٠	As on No. 39.
59	Ahmad-nagar	,,	Wt. 31 S. ·5	,,	As on No. 33.
60	(Ahmad)-nagar Shahr-i-(Humayun)	841	Wt. 72 S. ·65	,, but ٨٤١	As on No. 30. Top & right margins legible.
61	—	,,	Wt. 60 S. ·65	,,	As on No. 32.
62	Ahmad-(nagar)	842	Wt. 69 S. ·7	,, but ٨٤٢	As on No. 39.
63	—	,,	Wt. 63 S. ·65	,,	As on No. 32.
64	—	,,	Wt. 30 S. ·5	,,	,,

Æ No.	Mint	Date	Weight and size	Obverse	Reverse
					COPPER
65	—	842	Wt. 31 S. ·45	As on No. 30, but ٨٤٢	As on No. 32.
66	Ahmad-(nagar) Shahr-i-Humayun	843	Wt. 70 S. ·65	,, but (٨)٤٣	As on No. 34.
67	Ahmad-(nagar)	,,	Wt. 32 S. ·5	,,	As on No. 39.
68	(Ahmad-nagar) Shahr-i-Humayun	844	Wt. 72 S. ·65	,, but ٨٤٤	As on No. 30. Top & left margins legible.
69	—	845	Wt. 70 S. ·6	,, but ٨٤٥	As on No. 32.
70	Ahmad-(nagar)	(8)45	Wt. 55 S. ·6	,, but (٨)٤٥	As on No. 39.
71	— Shahr	845	Wt. 37 S. ·55	As on No. 69.	As on No. 30. Top margin legible.

Æ No.	Mint	Date	Weight and size	Obverse	Reverse
				COPPER	
72	Ahmad-(nagar) (Shahr-i-) Humayun	(8)46	Wt. 67 S. ·7	As on No. 30, but (٨)٤٦	As on No. 45.
73	— Shahr-i-Humayun	846	Wt. 63 S. ·6	,, but ٨٤٦	As on No. 68.
74	Ahmad-nagar Shahr-i-Humayun	835	Wt. 134 S. ·8	الدّنيا ناصـــر ٨٣٣ والدّين	As on No. 30. Pl. I.
75	Ahmad-nagar (Shahr-i-) Humayun	827	Wt. 120 S. ·75	السلطان الاعظم الدنيا و ناصـــر ٨٢٧ الدّين	,,
76	Ahmad-(nagar) Shahr-i-Humayun	(8)30	Wt. 111 S. ·8	,, but (٨)٣٠	As on No. 34.
77	Ahmad-(nagar) Shahr-i-Humayun	(8)31	Wt. 139 S. ·8	,, but (٨)٣١	As on No. 30.
78	Ahmad-nagar	837	Wt. 142 S. ·75	,, but ٨٣٧	As on No. 33. Pl. I.

Æ No.	Mint	Date	Weight and size	Obverse	Reverse
				COPPER	
79	Ahmad-nagar Shahr-i-Humayun	837	Wt. 136 S. ·75	As on No. 75, but ٨٣٧	As on No. 30.
80	(Ahmad-nagar) Shahr-i-Humayun	838	Wt. 144 S. ·75	,, but ٨٣٨	As on No. 71.
81	Ahmad-(nagar) Shahr-i-(Humayun)	,,	Wt. 135 S. ·8	,,	As on No. 39.
81a	—	,,	Wt. 65·5 S. ·65	As on No. 80.	As on No. 32. *I.M.C. No. 5.*
82	(Ahmad-nagar) Shahr-i-Humayun	839	Wt. 148 S. ·8	السلطان الاعظم الدُنيا وا ناصــــــر الدين ٨٣٩	As on No. 68. Pl. I.
83	Ahmad-nagar Shahr-i-Humayun	(8)39	Wt. 144 S. ·8	As on No. 75, but (٨)٣٩	As on No. 30.
84	Ahmad-nagar Shahr-i-(Humayun)	840	Wt. 141 S. ·75	,, but ٨٤٠	,, Left margin illegible.

Æ No.	Mint	Date	Weight and size	Obverse	Reverse
				COPPER	
85	(Ahmad-nagar)	840	Wt. 135 S. ·8	As on No. 75, but ٨٤٠	As on No. 32.
86	Ahmad-nagar Shahr-i-(Humayun)	841	Wt. 147 S. ·75	,, but ٨٤١	As on No. 84.
87	(Ahmad) nagar Shahr-i-(Humayun)	,,	Wt. 141 S. ·75	,,	As on No. 60.
88	Ahmad-(nagar) Shahr-i-Humayun	,,	Wt. 131 S. ·75	,,	As on No. 34.
89	Ahmad-nagar Shahr-i-Humayun	842	Wt. 147 S. ·75	,, but ٨٤٢	As on No. 30.
90	— Shahr-i-(Humayun)	,,	Wt. 129 S. ·75	,,	As on No. 71.
91	Ahmad-(nagar) Shahr-i-Humayun	843	Wt. 147 S. ·75	,, but ٨٤٣	As on No. 34.

Pl. I.

Æ No.	Mint	Date	Weight and size	Obverse	Reverse
				COPPER	
92	Ahmad-nagar	843	Wt. 143 S. ·75	As on No. 75, but ۸۴۳	As on No. 33.
93	Ahmad-nagar Shahr-i-(Humayun)	844	Wt. 144 S. ·75	„ but ۸۴۴	As on No. 84.
94	—	„	Wt. 71 S. ·6	„	As on No. 32.
95	Ahmad-(nagar) (Shahr-i-) Humayun	845	Wt. 145 S. ·75	„ but ۸۴۵	As on No. 45.
96	Ahmad-nagar Shahr-i-Humayun	„	Wt. 138 S. ·7	„	As on No. 30.
97	(Ahmad) nagar Shahr-i-(Humayun)	„	Wt. 134 S. ·7	„	As on No. 60.
98	Ahmad-nagar Shahr-i-(Humayun)	846	Wt. 144 S. ·65	„ but ۸۴۶	As on No. 84.

Æ No.	Mint	Date	Weight and size	Obverse	Reverse
				COPPER	
99	Ahmad- nagar Shahr-i- Humayun	846	Wt. 140 S. ·7	As on No. 75, but ٨٥٦	As on No. 30.
100	Ahmad- nagar	,,	Wt. 134 S. ·7	,,	As on No. 33.
101	Ahmad- (nagar) (Shahr-i-) Humayun	?	Wt. 68 S. ·65	,, but no date.	As on No. 45.

MUHAMMAD SHÁH II.

Æ No.	Mint	Date	Weight and size	Obverse	Reverse
102	—	(8)46	Wt. 142 S. ·7	السلطان (الاعظم) غيا الدنيا ـــث والدين	ابو المحامد شاه محـــمد السلطان (٨)٤٦ Pl. I.
103	—	846	Wt. 135 S. ·7	,,	,, Pl. I.
104	—	—	Wt. 66 S. ·6	غيا الدنيا ـــث والدين	,, but no date
105	—	846	Wt. 217 S. ·85	شاه باد غيا الدين محمد ـــث سكة سلطان ٨٤٦	و باد مهر ماه گردون قرص ـــد تابدار الظفر Pl. I.

Æ No.	Mint	Date	Weight and size	Obverse	Reverse
					COPPER
106	—	847	Wt. 220 S. ·9	As on No. 105, but date ۸۴۷	باد مهر و ماه گردون قرص تابد از الضر Pl. I.
107	—	,,	Wt. 207 S. ·9	,,	,,
108	—	,,	Wt. 197 S. ·8	,,	,,
109	—	848	Wt. 211 S. ·8	,, but date ۸۴۸	,, but باد written like this 
110	—	,,	Wt. 207 S. ·9	,,	As on No. 106.
111	—	849	Wt. 218 S. ·8	,, but date ۸۴۹	,,
112	—	850	Wt. 209 S. ·85	,, but date ۸۵۰	,,

Æ No.	Mint	Date	Weight and size	Obverse	Reverse
				COPPER	
113	—	852	Wt. 217 S. ·8	As on No. 105, but date ٨٥٢	As on No. 106.
114	—	853	Wt. 218· S. ·8	,, but date ٨٥٣	,,
115	—	854	Wt. 218 S. ·8	,, but date ٨٥٤	,, but Circle over ر of گردون
116	—	—	Wt. 195 S. ·7	,, but date illegible.	As on No. 106.
117	—	—	Wt. 146 S. ·8	,, but date not clear	,,
118	—	846	Wt. 72 S. ·65	As on No. 104.	السلطان شاه محمد ٨٤٦ Pl. I.
119	—	852	Wt. 69 S. ·65	,,	السلطان محمد شاه (٨)٥٢

Æ No.	Mint	Date	Weight and size	Obverse	Reverse
					COPPER
119a	—	853	Wt. 72 S. ·65	As on No. 104.	As on No. 119, but date ٨٥٣ *J.A.S.B., Vol. LVIII, p. 1.*
120	—	854	Wt. 71 S. ·6	,,	,, but date ٨٥٤
121	—	(8)51	Wt. 28 S. ·5	,,	,, but date (٨)٥١
122	—	847	Wt. 69 S. ·65	,,	محمد شاه السلطان ٨٤٧ Pl.
123	—	848	Wt. 72 S. ·6	,,	,, but date ٨٤٨
123a	—	84x	Wt. 34 S. ·55	,,	,, but date ٨٤x *Mr. R. Antani's Collection.*
124	—	850	Wt. 69 S. ·6	,,	,, but date ٨٥٠

Æ No.	Mint	Date	Weight and size	Obverse	Reverse
				COPPER	
125	—	853	Wt. 68 S. ·6	As on No. 104.	As on No. 122, but date ۸۵۳
125a	—	(8)54	,,	,,	,, *W.M.R.*
126	—	—	Wt. 33 S. ·5	,,	,, but no date.
127	—	—	Wt. 31 S. ·5	,,	,, but السلطان written differently.

AḤMAD SHÁH II.

AR					
				SILVER	
127a	—	—	Wt. 174 S. 1.	السلطان الاعظم الدنيا والدين قطب ابو المظفر	احمد شاه بن محمد شاه بن احمد شاه بن محمد شاه بن مظفر شاه خلد خلافته Pl. II. *N.C. 5th Series, Vol. IV, p. 104.*

Æ No.	Mint	Date	Weight and size	Obverse	Reverse
				COPPER	
128	—	855	Wt. 216 S. ·8	قطب الدنيا والدين ابو المظفر	السلطان شاه احمد ٨٥٥ Circle over ح of Ahmad as in case of Ahmad Shah I's Coins. Pl. II.
129	—	,,	Wt. 209 S. ·8	,,	,,
130	—	,,	Wt. 186 S. ·8	,,	,,
131	—	(8)5x	Wt. 157 S. ·7	,,	,, but date (٨)٥x
132	—	855	Wt. 144 S. ·75	,,	As on No. 128.
133	—	(8)56	Wt. 146 S. ·7	,,	,, but date (٨)٥٦
134	—	856	Wt. 140 S. ·75	,,	,, but date ٨٥٦

Æ No.	Mint	Date	Weight and size	Obverse	Reverse
				COPPER	
135	—	858	Wt. 143 S. ·65	As on No. 128.	As on No. 128, but date ٨٥٨
136	—	859	Wt. 148 S. ·7	,,	,, but date ٨٥٩
137	—	,,	Wt. 140 S. ·7	,,	,,
138	—	(8)5x	Wt. 128 S. ·75	,,	As on No. 131.
139	—	—	Wt. 112 S. ·7	,,	As on No. 128, but date illegible.
140	—	85x	Wt. 73 S. ·6	,,	,, but date ٨٥x
141	—	—	Wt. 72 S. ·65	,,	,, but no date

Æ No.	Mint	Date	Weight and size	Obverse	Reverse
				COPPER	
142	—	—	Wt. 62 S. ·65	As on No. 128.	As on No. 128, but no date.
143	—	—	Wt. 56 S. ·65	,,	,,
				BILLON	
B 144	—	(8)56	Wt. 139 S. ·7	قطب الدنيا والدين احمد شاه السلطان	الخليفه المومنين امير خان خلافته ... ٦ع(٨) Pl. II.
145	—	(8)59	Wt. 146 S. ·7	,,	,, but date (٨)ع٩
146	—	(8)60	Wt. 145 S. ·7	,,	,, but date (٨)٦٠ above خلافته
147	—	861	Wt. 145 S. ·7	,,	,, but date ٨٦١
148	—	862	Wt. 145 S. ·65	,,	,, but date ٨٦٢

B No.	Mint	Date	Weight and size	Obverse	Reverse
				BILLON	
149	—	863	Wt. 141 S. ·7	As on No. 144.	As on No. 146, but date ٨٦٣
				COPPER	
Æ 150	—	85x	Wt 69 S. ·6	الدنیا قطب والدین	As on No. 128, but date ٨٤x
151	—	—	Wt. 70 S. ·65	,,	As on No. 141. Pl. II.
152	—	—	Wt. 35 S. ·5	,,	As on No. 139.
152a	—	—	Wt. 18 S. ·5	,,	,, Gad : Coll:

MAHMŪD SHÁH I.

B No.	Mint	Date	Weight and size	Obverse	Reverse
				GOLD	
AV 152b	—	914	Wt. 183·6 S. ·85	الرحمن الواثق بتائید الفتح ناصر الدنیا والدین ابو	In double square السلطان شاه شاه محمود بن محمد Bottom margin ٩١٤ Pl. II. *N.C. 5th Series, Vol. IV, p. 104.*

Æ No.	Mint	Date	Weight and size	Obverse	Reverse
				SILVER	
152e	—	(8)69?	Wt. 172 S. ·9	الواثق بالله المنان الدنيا والدين نـاصـــر ابوالفتح	محمود شاه ابن محمد شاه ابن احمد شاه ابن محمد شاه ابن مظفر شاه السلطان ٦٥(٨) *B.B.R.A.S.* Pl. II.
153	Mustafa- (bad) (Shahr-i-) A'zam	884	Wt. 63 S. ·6	(الدنيا) و نـاصـــر الدين ابوالفتح ٨٨۴	In square السلطان شاه محمود *Margins*:— Right اعظم Top مصطفٰى Pl. II.
154	Mustafa- (bad)	885	Wt. 66 S. ·55	,, but date ٨٨۵	,, but top margin مصطفٰى
155	Mustafa- bad	886	Wt. 66 S. ·6	,, but date ٨٨٦	,, but *Margins*:— Top مصطفٰى Left باد
156	Mustafa- (bad) (Shahr-i-) A'zam	(8)88	Wt. 65 S. ·5	,, but date (٨)٨٨	,,
157	—	x8x	Wt. 32 S. ·45	,, but date -٨-	,, Margins illegible.
158	Mustafa- (bad) (Shahr-i-) A'zam	884	Wt. 64 S. ·55	الدنيا نـاصـــر والدين ٨٨۴ ابوالفتح	As on No. 153.

Æ No.	Mint	Date	Weight and size	Obverse	Reverse
				SILVER	
159	Mustafa-(bad) Shahr-i-A'zam	(8)85	Wt. 65 S. ·6	As on No. 158, but date (٨)٨٤	As on No. 153, but *Margins :—* Bottom شهر Right اعظم Top مصطفے
160	(Mustafa-bad) Shahr-i-A'zam	886	Wt. 66 S. ·65	,, but date ٨٨٦	,, but *Margins :—* Bottom شهر Right اعظم
161	—	,,	Wt. 66 S. ·55	,,	As on No. 157.
162	— Shahr-i-(A'zam)	(8)86	Wt. 48 S. ·55	,,	As on No. 153, but bottom margin شهر
163	— Shahr-i-(A'zam)	887	Wt. 66 S. ·6	,, but date ٨٨٧	,,
164	— Shahr-i-(A'zam)	(8)87	Wt. 57 S. ·55	,,	,,
165	—	888	Wt. 66 S. ·55	,, but date ٨٨٨	As on No. 157.
166	—	(8)89	Wt. 66 S. ·55	,, but date (٨)٨٩	,,

Æ No.	Mint	Date	Weight and size	Obverse	Reverse
				SILVER	
167	—	896	Wt. 66 S. ·5	As on No. 158, but date ٨٩٦	As on No. 157.
168	—	897	Wt. 66 S. ·55	,, but date ٨٩٧	,,
169	—	898	Wt. 66 S. ·55	,, but date ٨٩٨	,,
170	—	(8)99	Wt. 66 S. ·5	,, but date (٨)٩٩	,,
171	—	900	Wt. 65 S. ·5	,, but date ٩٠٠	,,
172	—	(9)01	Wt. 66 S. ·5	,, but date (٩)٠١	,,
173	—	901	Wt. 33 S. ·4	,,	,,
173a	—	903	Wt. 65 S. ·5	,, but date (٩)٠٣	,,

I.M.C. No. 34.

AR No.	Mint	Date	Weight and size	Obverse	Reverse
				SILVER	
174	—	904	Wt. 65 S. ·5	As on No. 158, but date ۹۰۴	As on No. 157.
174a	—	905	Wt. 65·4	,, but date ۹۰۵	,, *Fitzwilliam Museum, Cambridge.*
175	—	(9)07	Wt. 65 S. ·55	,, but date (۹)۰۷	,,
176	Mustafa-bad Shahr-i-A'zam	905	Wt. 66 S. ·65	,, but date ۹۰۵	As on No. 153, but *Margins:—* Top شهر Left اعظم Bottom مصطفے Right باد
177	,,	906	Wt. 62 S. ·6	,, but date ۹۰۶	,, but right margin missing.
178	,,	,,	Wt. 66 S. ·7	,, but within dotted circle	,, but within dotted circle. Pl. II.
179	,,	,,	Wt. 66 S. ·6	As on No. 177.	,, but *Margins:—* Bottom شهر Right اعظم Top مصطفے Left باد

Æ No.	Mint	Date	Weight and size	Obverse	Reverse
				SILVER	
180	Mustafa-bad Shahr-i-A'zam	906	Wt. 45 S. ·6	As on No. 177.	As on No. 179, but defaced.
181	—	891	Wt. 80 S. ·6	السلطان الاعظم الدنيا ناصر والدين ۸۹۱ ابوالفتح	In a circle. السلطان شاه محمود Margins illegible. Pl. II.
182	Mustafa ?	(8)91	Wt. 80 S. ·6	,,	,,
183	Mustafa-bad Shahr-i-A'zam	894	Wt. 65 S. ·6	,, but within dotted circle.	As on No. 178. Pl. II.
184	,,	,,	Wt. 65 S. ·6	,,	,,
185	Mustafa-(bad) (Shahr-i-) A'zam	(8)94	Wt. 63 S. ·55	As on No. 181, but date (۸)۹۴	As on No. 176, but top and right margins missing.
186	Mustafa-bad Shahr-i-A'zam	,,	Wt. 31·5 S. ·4	As on No. 183.	,, Pl. II.

AR No.	Mint	Date	Weight and size	Obverse	Reverse
				SILVER	
186a	(Shahr-i-) A'zam Mustafa- (bad)	900 ?	Wt. 42 S. ·5	السلطان الاعظم الفـــــتح ناصر الدنيا ابو والدين ٩٠(٠)	In square with peake[d] sides. السلطان شاه محمود Right margin اعظم Top مصطفى *A.N.S. No. 242*
187	Mustafa- bad Shahr-i- A'zam	905	Wt. 89 S. ·75	In a dotted circle. السلطان الاعظم الفـــــتح ناصرالدنيا والدين ابو ٩٠٥	In a square. السلطان شاه محمود Margins as on No. 17[6] Pl. I[I]
188	,,	906	Wt. 88 S. ·75	,,	,, but *Margins* :— Bottom شهر Left اعظم Top مصطفى Right باد
189	—	908	Wt. 82 S. ·65	السلطان الاعظم الفـــــتح ناصر الدنيا وابو الدين ٩٠٨	In square with peake[d] sides. السطان شاه محمود Margins illegible.
190	Mustafa- (bad) (Shahr-i-) A'zam	909	Wt. 88 S. ·7	,, but date ٩٠٩	,, but *Margins* :— Right اعظم Top مصطفى Pl. I
191	—	910	Wt. 88 S. ·65	,, but date ٩١٠	As on No. 189.
192	—	911	Wt. 87 S. ·65	,, but date ٩١١	,,

Æ No.	Mint	Date	Weight and size	Obverse	Reverse
				SILVER	
192a	—	911	Wt. 43 S. ·55	As on No. 192.	As on No. 189. *A.N.S. No. 245.*
193	Mustafa-(bad) (Shahr-i-) A'zam	912	Wt. 87 S. ·65	As on No. 189, but date ٩١٢	As on No. 190.
194	,,	913	Wt. 82 S. ·65	,, but date ٩١٣	,,
195	,,	914	Wt. 82 S. ·65	,, but date ٩١٤	,,
196	(Mustafa-) bad	915	Wt. 82 S. ·65	,, but date ٩١٥	As on No. 189, but left margin باد
197	—	916	Wt. 78 S. ·65	,, but date ٩١٦	As on No. 189.
198	—	,,	Wt. 82 S. ·65	,, but date ٩١٦ in the centre.	,,
199	—	,,	Wt. 41 S. ·5	,,	,,

AR. No.	Mint	Date	Weight and size	Obverse	Reverse
				SILVER	
200	—	917	Wt. 83 S. ·65	As on No. 198, but date ۹۱۷	As on No. 189.
201	—	,,	Wt. 77 S. ·6	,,	,,
202	(Muhammadabad) Shahr-i-Mukarram	891	Wt. 88 S. ·6	As on No. 181.	شاه محمود السلطان شهر مکرّم محمد آباد
202a	?	892	Wt. 86 S. ·55	د ه محمو شا السلطان	سلطا ضرب ماقلند (؟) سنه ۸۹۲ *P. P. M. No. 2.*
203	Muhammadabad Shahr-i-Mukarram	893	Wt. 87 S. ·6	As on No. 181, but date ۸۹۳	As on No. 202. Pl. II.
204	(Muhammadabad) Shahr-i-Mukarram	,,	Wt. 84 S. ·5	,,	,,
205	,,	(8)94	Wt. 83 S. ·5	As on No. 185.	,,
206	Muhammadabad Shahr-i-Mukarram	,,	Wt. 88 S. ·55	As on No. 187, but without dotted circle.	د ه محمو شا السلطان شهر مکرّم محمد آباد (۸)۹۴

Æ No.	Mint	Date	Weight and size	Obverse	Reverse
				SILVER	
207	Muham-madabad Shahr-i-Mukarram	894	Wt. 86 S. ·55	As on No. 206.	As on No. 206.
208	,,	,,	Wt. 44 S. ·5	As on No. 187, but in a plain circle.	,, Pl. II.
209	,,	,,	Wt. 85 S. ·6	,,	In a square السلطان شاه محمود *Margins* :— Right شهر مكرّم Top محمد Left آباد Bottom ٨٩٤
210	,,	,,	Wt. 87 S. ·65	,,	In a square السلطان محمود شاه *Margins* :— Right شهر مكرّم Top محمد Left آباد Bottom سنة ٨٩٤ Pl. II.
211	,,	895	Wt. 88 S. ·65	,,	In a square السلطان شاه محمود Margins as on No. 210, but date ٨٩٥
212	,,	896	Wt. 87 S. ·65	,,	,, but date ٨٩٦

AR No.	Mint	Date	Weight and size	Obverse	Reverse
				SILVER	
213	Muham-madabad Shahr-i-Mukarram	897	Wt. 87 S. ·75	As on No. 187.	In a square السلطان محمود شاه Margins as on No. 210, but date ۸۹۷
214	,,	,,	Wt. 80 S. ·75	As on No. 208.	,,
215	,,	898	Wt. 87 S. ·7	,,	As on No. 211, but date ۸۹۸
216	,,	,,	Wt. 43 S. ·6	As on No. 187.	As on No. 213, but date ۸۹۸
217	Muham-mad(abad) Shahr-i Mukarram	899	Wt. 87 S. ·75	As on No. 208.	In a square السلطان شاه محمود Margins as on No. 210, but left margin missing and date ۸۹۹
218	Muham-madabad Shahr-i-Mukarram	,,	Wt. 84 S. ·7	,,	,,
219	(Muham-mad)abad (Shahr-i-Mukarram)	,,	Wt. 43 S. ·55	,,	,, but right and top margins missing.

AR No.	Mint	Date	Weight and size	Obverse	Reverse
					SILVER
220	Muham-madabad Shahr-i-Mukarram	900	Wt. 87 S. ·65	As on No. 208.	As on No. 217, but margins as on No. 210 and date ٩٠٠
221	Muham-madabad	901	Wt. 87 S. ·7	,,	,, but right margin missing and date ٩٠١
222	Muham-madabad Shahr-i-Mukarram	902	Wt. 88 S. ·7	As on No. 187.	Area as on No. 187, but margins as on No. 210 and date ٩٠٢
223	Muham-mad(abad) Shahr-i-Mukarram	,,	Wt. 83 S. ·65	,,	,, but left margin missing.
224	(Muham-mad)abad	903	Wt. 88 S. ·65	As on No. 208.	In a square السلطان شاه محمود Margins as on No. 219.
225	Muham-madabad Shahr-i-Mukarram	904	Wt. 88 S. ·7	,,	In a square السلطان شاه محمود Margins as on No. 210, but date ٩٠٤
226	(Muham-madabad) Shahr-i-Mukarram	906	Wt. 88 S. ·65	,,	,, but top and left margins missing.

AR No.	Mint	Date	Weight and size	Obverse	Reverse
					SILVER
226a	—	908	Wt. 87·5 S. ·6	As on No. 208.	Area as on No. 225. Bottom margin has date ٩٠٨ *A.N.S. No. 236.*
227	Muhammadabad Shahr-i-Mukarram	896	Wt. 166 S. ·85	,,	As on No. 213, but date ٨٩٦
227a	,,	897	Wt. 176 S. ·85	,,	,, but date ٨٩٧ *A.N.S. No. 227.*
228	(Muhammadabad) Shahr-i-Mukarram	905	Wt. 172 S. ·75	,,	,, but top and left margins missing and date ٩٠ع
228a	Muhammadabad (Shahr-i-Mukarram)	906	Wt. 171 S. ·8	,,	,, but top and left margins clear and date ٩٠٦ *I.M.C. No. 14.*
229	Muhammadabad Shahr-i-Mukarram	908	Wt. 170 S. ·75	,,	As on No. 225, but date ٩٠٨
229a	,,	901	Wt. 88.3 S. ·68	As on No. 187.	In a square محمود شاه السلطان *Margins*:— Left آباد (?) Bottom ٩٠١ *P.C.C.A., p. 219, No. 8.*

Æ No.	Mint	Date	Weight and size	Obverse	Reverse
					SILVER
229b	—	902	Wt. 86 S. ·65	As on No. 208.	In a square شاه محمود السلطان Margins missing. *A.N.S. No. 232.*
230	Muhammadabad Shahr-i-Mukarram	907	Wt. 175 S. ·75	As on No. 187.	In a square شاه محمود السلطان Margins as on No. 210, but date ۹۰۷
230a	—	,,	Wt. 86	,,	,, but date 907 in reverse ۷۰۹ *W.M.R.*
231	—	—	Wt. 88 S. ·65	As on No. 208.	Area as on No. 230 & margins missing.
232	—	—	Wt. 70 S. ·65	,,	,,
233	Muhammad(abad) Shahr-i-Mukarram	901	Wt. 172 S. ·7	,,	In a square السلطان شاه شاه محمود بن محمد *Margins:—* Right شهر مكرم Top محمد Bottom ۹۰۱

Æ No.	Mint	Date	Weight and size	Obverse	Reverse
				SILVER	
233a	Muham-madabad (Shahr-i-Mukarram)	—	Wt. 88·5 S. ·67	As on No. 208.	Area as on No. 233, but *Margins :—* Top محمد Left آباد and no date. *P.C.C.A., p. 220, No. 10.*
234	—	909	Wt. 88 S. ·65	As on No. 206.	,, Bottom margin ٩٠٩
235	Muham-madabad Shahr-i-Mukarram	910	Wt. 175 S. ·75	As on No. 187.	,, but Left margin آباد Bottom ٩١٠ سنة Pl. III.
236	,,	911	Wt. 165 S. ·85	,,	In double square السلطان شاه محمود بن محمد *Margins :—* Right شهر مكرّم Top محمد Left آباد Bottom ٩١١ سنه Pl. III.
237	— Shahr-i-Mukarram	912	Wt. 162 S. ·75	As on No. 206.	,, but Right margin شهر مكرّم and bottom ٩١٢ سنة
238	—	,,	Wt. 161 S. ·8	As on No. 187.	In double square السلطان شاه محمود بن محمد Bottom margin ٩١٢

AR No.	Mint	Date	Weight and size	Obverse	Reverse
				SILVER	
239	—	912	Wt. 82 S. ·7	As on No. 187.	As on No. 237.
239a	—	916	Wt. 165 S. ·75	As on No. 206.	,, but bottom margin ٩١۴ *I.M.C. No. 18.*
240	—	917	Wt. 157 S. ·8	As on No. 208.	Area as on No. 236. Margins illegible. Bottom ٩١٧ سنة
241	—	—	Wt. 41 S. ·5	,,	,, but no margins.
242	—	—	Wt. 38 S. ·5	,,	,,
243	Muham- madabad alias Cham- pa(nir)	—	Wt. 176 S. ·8	,,	In scalloped circle شاه محمود السلطان Top and left margins محمدآباد عرف چانپا(نير) Pl. III.
244	Muham- madabad Shahr-i- Mukarram	900	Wt. 87 S. ·7	As on No. 187, but in a scalloped circle.	In square with peaked sides. السلطان شاه محمود *Margins* :— Right شهر مکرم Top محمد آباد Bottom ٩٠٠

SILVER

AR No.	Mint	Date	Weight and size	Obverse	Reverse
245	Muham- madabad alias Cham- panir Shahr-i- Mukarram	901	Wt. 88 S. ·7	As on No. 238.	Area as on No. 244, but *Margins* :— Right شهر مُكرّم Top محمد آباد Left (عُرف)چانپانیر Bottom ۹۰۱ سنة
246	Muham- madabad alias (Cham- panir) Shahr-i- Mukarram	,,	Wt. 83 S. ·7	,,	,, but left margin missing.
247	Muham- madabad alias Cham- panir Shahr-i- Mukarram	902	Wt. 84 S. ·7	As on No. 206.	,, but date ۹۰۲ in upside-down form.
248	Muham- madabad Shahr-i- Mukarram	,,	Wt. 88 S. ·7	,,	As on No. 244, but date ۹۰۲ in upside-down form.
249	Muham- madabad Shahr-i- Mukarram	90x	Wt. 43 S. ·55	,,	,, but *Margins* :— Right شهر Top مُكرّم Left محمد آباد Bottom ۹۰x سنة
250	Muham- madabad alias Cham- panir Shahr-i- Mukarram	902	Wt. 88 S. ·7	,,	In square with peaked sides السلطان محمود شاه *Margins* :— Right ضرب شهر مُكرّم Top محمد آباد Left عُرف چانپانیر Bottom ۹۰۲ سنة

AR No.	Mint	Date	Weight and size	Obverse	Reverse
				SILVER	
251	Muhammadabad alias Champanir Shahr-i-Mukarram	903	Wt. 86 S. ·7	As on No. 206.	As on No. 250, but date ۹۰۳ Pl. III.
252	— Champaner ? Shahr-i-Mukarram	,,	Wt. 88 S. ·7	,,	In hexagon شاه محمود السلطان *Margins* :— Right ضرب شهر مکرم Bottom ۹۰۳ سنة Pl. III.
253	—	—	Wt. 43 S. .5	,,	In hexagon شاه محمود السلطان
254	Dîb Khittāh	900	Wt. 86 S. ·8	As on No. 187.	In a square السلطان شاه محمود *Margins* :— Left خطة Top دیب Right سنه Bottom ۹۰۰ outer linear and dotted circle.
255	,,	,,	Wt. 87 S. ·7	,,	,, Pl. III.
256	,,	,,	Wt. 42 S. ·55	,,	,,

AR. No.	Mint	Date	Weight and size	Obverse	Reverse
				SILVER	
257	—	—	Wt. 78 S. ·6	As on No. 206.	In scalloped circle السلطان سا ه محمود
				COPPER	
Æ 258	—	863	Wt. 144 S. ·7	الدنيا و ناصر الدين ابوالفتح محمود شاه	اخ شاه قطب محمد شاه بن السلطا ٨٦٣ Pl. III
259	—	,,	Wt. 139 S. ·7	و الدنيا الدين ناصر ابوالفتح محمود شاه السلطان	الخليفه المومنين امير خلد خلافته ٨٦٣ Pl. III
260	—	xx3	Wt. 72 S. ·55	الدنيا ناصر والدين	ابو الفتح محمود شاه السلطا xx٣
261	—	868	Wt. 134 S. ·75	السلطان الاعظم الدنيا ناصر والدين	,, but date ٨٦٨ Pl. III
262	—	869	Wt. 145 S. ·65	,,	,, but date ٨٦٩

Æ No.	Mint	Date	Weight and size	Obverse	Reverse
				COPPER	
263	—	869	Wt. 142 S. ·65	As on No. 261.	As on No. 262.
264	—	(8)70	Wt. 143 S. ·65	,,	As on No. 260, but date (٨)٧٠
265	—	871	Wt. 147 S. ·6	,,	,, but date ٨٧١
266	—	872	Wt. 142 S. ·65	,,	,, but date ٨٧٢
267	—	(8)73	Wt. 145 S. ·65	,,	,, but date (٨)٧٣
268	—	(8)81	Wt. 145 S. ·7	,,	,, but date (٨)٨١
268a	—	897	Wt. 142·5 S. ·65	,, but date ٨٩٧	,, but date on other side. *A.N.S. No. 65.*
269	—	(8)62	Wt. 138 S. ·7	As on No. 261.	شاه محمود بن محمد شاه السلطا (٨)٦٢

Æ No.	Mint	Date	Weight and size	Obverse	Reverse
					COPPER
270	—	(8)64	Wt. 144 S. ·7	As on No. 261, but date (٨)٦٤ in the ن of الدين	محمود شاه محمد شاه بن السلطان Pl. III.
271	—	x65	Wt. 141 S. ·65	,, but date (٨)٦٥	,,
272	—	—	Wt. 63 S. ·6	As on No. 261.	,,
273	—	(8)64	Wt. 141 S. ·7	الدنيا ناصر والدين ابو الفتح	محمود شاه محمد شاه بن السلطان (٨)٦٤
274	—	(8)65	Wt. 146 S. ·7	,,	,, but date (٨)٦٥
275	—	,,	Wt. 137 S. ·65	,,	,,
276	—	(8)66	Wt. 142 S. ·7	,,	As on No. 273, but date (٨)٦٦
277	—	867	Wt. 145 S. ·7	,,	,, but date ٨٦٧ Pl. III.

Æ No.	Mint	Date	Weight and size	Obverse	Reverse
				COPPER	
278	—	(8)67	Wt. 139 S. ·7	As on No. 273.	As on No. 273, but date (٨) ٢٧= (٨) ٦٧
279	—	,,	Wt. 134 S. ·7	,,	As on No. 277.
280	—	(8)69	Wt. 133 S. ·65	,,	As on No. 273, but date (٨)٦٩
281	—	883	Wt. 82 S. ·6	As on No. 158, but date ٨٨٣	As on No. 270.
282	—	(8)84	Wt. 80 S. ·55	,,	,,
283	—	(8)85	Wt. 84 S. ·6	As on No. 159.	,,
284	—	887	Wt. 82 S. ·55	As on No. 163.	,,
285	—	(8)88	Wt. 84 S. ·6	As on No. 165.	,,

Æ No.	Mint	Date	Weight and size	Obverse	Reverse
				COPPER	
286	—	889	Wt. 84 S. ·55	As on No. 166, but date ٨٨٩ below الدين	As on No. 270.
287	—	(8) 91	Wt. 65 S. ·6	الدنيا ناصر والدين (٨)٩١	السلطان محمد شاه بن محمود شاه
288	—	—	Wt. 50 S. ·5	As on No. 273.	As on No. 270.
289	—	—	Wt. 35 S. ·5	الدنيا ناصر والدين	,, Pl. III.
290	—	864	Wt. 74 S. ·55	As on No. 287, but date ٨٦٤	السلطان شاه محمود
291	—	—	Wt. 34 S. ·4	As on No. 273.	,,
292	—	880	Wt. 72 S. ·6	As on No. 287, but date ٨٨٠	محمود شاه السلطان Pl. III.
293	—	(8)81	Wt. 70 S. ·6	,, but date (٨)٨١	,,

Æ No.	Mint	Date	Weight and size	Obverse	Reverse
				COPPER	
294	—	xx3	Wt. 41 S. ·5	As on No. 287, but date xx٣	As on No. 292.
294a	—	884	Wt. 73·5 S. ·6	,, but but date (٨)٨٤	,, *A.N.S. No. 73.*
295	—	(8)85	Wt. 73 S. ·6	,, but date (٨)٨٥	محمود شاه السلطان
296	—	888	Wt. 70 S. ·55	,, but date ٨٨٨	,,
297	—	889	Wt. 69 S. ·55	,, but date ٨٨٩ at the bottom	,,
298	—	—	Wt. 66 S. ·55	As on No. 273.	As on No. 292.
299	—	880	Wt. 72 S. ·55	As on No. 153, but date (٨) ٨٠	محمود شاه السلطان ٨٨٠
300	—	—	Wt. 34 S. ·45	,, but date illegible.	As on No. 295.

Æ No.	Mint	Date	Weight and size	Obverse	Reverse
				COPPER	
301	—	—	Wt. 27 S. ·45	As on No. 289.	As on No. 295.
302	—	—	Wt. 18 S. ·35	,,	,,
303	Mustafa-bad Shahr-i-A'zam	(8)71	Wt. 213 S. ·75	السلطان الاعظم الدنيا و ناصـــــر الدين ٧١(٨)	Area as on No. 153, but *Margins* :— Bottom شهر Right اعظم Top مصطفےٰ Left باد Pl. III.
304	,,	880	Wt. 214 S. ·7	,, but date ٨٨٠	,,
305	,,	881	Wt. 219 S. ·75	,, but date ٨٨١	,, Pl. III.
306	Mustafa-bad (Shahr-i-) A'zam	882	Wt. 219 S. ·75	,, but date ٨٨٢	,, but bottom margin missing.
307	Mustafa-bad	885	Wt. 212 S. ·7	,, but date ٨٨٥	,, but bottom and right margins missing.
308	Mustafa-bad (Shahr-i-) A'zam	886	Wt. 217 S. ·7	,, but date ٨٨٦	As on No. 306.

Æ No.	Mint	Date	Weight and size	Obverse	Reverse
				COPPER	
309	—	(8)86	Wt. 142 S. ·6	As on No. 308.	As on No. 157.
310	—	,,	Wt. 72 S. ·55	,,	,,
311	Mustafa-(bad) Shahr-i-A'zam	(8)87	Wt. 218 S. ·7	As on No. 303, but date (٨)٨٧	As on No. 303, but left margin missing.
312	(Mustafa-)bad Shahr-i-(A'zam)	(8)88	Wt. 218 S. ·7	,, but date (٨)٨٨	,, but right and top margins missing.
313	— (Shahr-i-) A'zam	888	Wt. 144 S. ·65	,,	,, but only right margin legible.
314	Mustafa-bad	889	Wt. 217 S. ·7	As on No. 303, but date (٨)٨٩	As on No. 307.
315	Mustafa-(bad) Shahr-i-A'zam	890	Wt. 219 S. ·7	,, but date ٨٩٠	As on No. 177.
316	(Mustafa-)bad Shahr-i-(A'zam)	891	Wt. 218 S. ·7	As on No. 268, but date ٨٩١	As on No. 176, but left and bottom margins missing.

Æ No.	Mint	Date	Weight and size	Obverse	Reverse
				COPPER	
317	—	(8)92	Wt. 147 S. ·6	As on No. 268, but date (٨)٩٢	As on No. 157.
318	Mustafa-(bad)	(8)93	Wt. 217 S. ·7	As on No. 303, but date (٨)٩٣	As on No. 303, but only top margin legible.
319	—	893	Wt. 144 S. ·65	(نا)صر الدّين ٨٩٣	As on No. 157.
320	(Mustafa-)bad Shahr-i-(A'zam)	(8)94	Wt. 217 S. ·7	As on No. 268, but date (٨)٩٤	As on No. 316.
				BILLON	
B 321	—	874	Wt. 113 S. ·65	As on No. 273.	In square area ن السلطا شاه محمود *In Margins* :— Top سنه Left اربع Bottom سبعين Right (ثما نمايته) Pl. III.
322	—	87x	Wt. 113 S. ·6	,,	,,
323	—	—	Wt. 113 S. ·6	,,	,, but margins illegible.
323a	—	873	—	,,	As on No. 324 below, but date in margin في سنه ثلث وسبعين و (ثمانمايته) *W.M.R.*

B No.	Mint	Date	Weight and size	Obverse	Reverse
					BILLON
324	—	877	Wt. 174 S. ·65	As on No. 273.	In circular area السلطان شاه محمود *In Margins* :— في سنه سبع سبعين وثمانماية Pl. III.
324a	—	878	Wt. 172 S. ·7	,,	,, but date في سنه ثمان سبعين وثمانماية *N.S., No. XVII, p. 132.*
325	Mustafa- bad Shahr-i- A'zam	879	Wt. 173 S. ·7	As on No. 155, but date ٨٧٩	,, *In Margins* :— شهر اعظم مصطفى باد Pl. III.
325a	(Mustafa- bad) Shahr-i- A'zam	880	Wt. 174·5 S. ·7	As on No. 273, but date ٨٨٠ at the bottom.	,, but without مصطفى باد *A.N.S., No. 66.*
326	Mustafa- bad (Shahr-i-) A'zam	881	Wt. 176 S. ·7	,, but date ٨٨١ at the bottom.	As on No. 325.
326a	Mustafa- bad Shahr-i- A'zam	,,	Wt. 160·5 S. ·7	As on No. 155, but date ٨٨١	,, *A.N.S., No. 67.*
327	Mustafa- bad	(8)81	Wt. 164 S. ·7	,,	,, but شهراعظم missing
328	Mustafa- bad Shahr-i- A'zam	,,	Wt. 151 S. ·7	,,	Area as on No. 324. *In Margins* :— ضرب شهر اعظم مصطفى باد

B No.	Mint	Date	Weight and size	Obverse	Reverse
				BILLON	
329	(Mustafa-bad) Shahr-i-A'zam	—	Wt. 172 S. ·7	As on No. 273.	As on No. 325.
Æ				**COPPER**	
329a	,,	878 ?	Wt. 115·5 S. ·6	As on No. 155, but date ٨٧٨ ?	Area as on No. 153, but *Margins* :— Bottom شهر Right اعظم *A.N.S. No. 84.*
330	— Shahr-i-(A'zam)	880	Wt. 215 S. ·75	,, but date ٨٨٠	,, but *Margins* :— Top ضرب Left شهر
331	Mustafa-bad Shahr-i-A'zam	881	Wt. 213 S. ·8	,, but date ٨٨١	,, but *Margins* :— Top ضرب Left شهر Bottom اعظم Right مصطفے اباد Pl. III.
332		882	Wt. 215 S. ·7	,, but date ٨٨٢	As on No. 303.
332a	,,	(8)85	Wt. 215.5 S. ·7	,, but date (٨)٨٥	,, *A.N.S. No. 75.*
333	—	886	Wt. 221 S. ·7	,, but date ٨٨٦	,, but only bottom margin legible.
334	—	887	Wt. 215 S. ·7	,, but date ٨٨٧	,,

Æ No.	Mint	Date	Weight and size	Obverse	Reverse
				COPPER	
335	—	x8x	Wt. 70 S. ·55	As on No. 157.	As on No. 157.
336	Mustafa-bad Shahr-i-A'zam.	—	Wt. 71 S. ·55	As on No. 153, but date illegible.	As on No. 303. Pl. III.
337	—	892	Wt. 216 S ·75	As on No. 155, but date ٨٩٢	As on No. 157.
338	—	891	Wt. 222 S. ·7	السلطان الاعظم الدنيا ناصـــر ٨٩١ والدين ابوالفتح	,,
339	Mustafa-(bad) (Shahr-i-) A'zam.	892	Wt. 221 S. ·75	,, but date ٨٩٢	As on No. 185.
340	—	(8)93	Wt. 144 S. ·6	As on No. 181, but date (٨)٩٣	As on No. 333.
341	Mustafa-(bad.)	894	Wt. 216 S. ·7	,, but date ٨٩٤	As on No. 185.
342	Mustafa-bad Shahr-i-A'zam.	(8)82	Wt. 171 S. ·7	As on No. 326, but date (٨)٨٢	السلطان شاه محمود في شهر اعظم مصطفى باد Pl. IV.

Æ No.	Mint	Date	Weight and size	Obverse	Reverse
				COPPER	
343	Mustafa-bad Shahr-i-A'zam.	883	Wt. 171 S. ·7	As on No. 158, but date ٨٨٣	As on No. 342.
344	„	884	Wt. 173 S. ·7	„	„
345	(Mustafa-bad) Shahr-i-A'zam.	(8)85	Wt. 170 S. ·65	As on No. 159.	„
346	„	(8)86	Wt. 174 S. ·65	As on No. 160.	„
347	Mustafa-bad Shahr-i-A'zam.	(8)87	Wt. 167 S. ·6	As on No. 164.	„
348	Mustafa-bad Shahr-i-A'zam.	(8)88	Wt. 170 S. ·65	As on No. 165.	„
349	(Mustafa-bad) Shahr-i-A'zam.	889	Wt. 173 S. ·6	As on No. 158, but date ٨٨٩ in reverse form.	„
350	Mustafa-(bad)	888	Wt. 139 S. ·6	مصطفیٰ ٨٨٨ ناصر الدنیا والدین	Area as on No. 153, but defaced.

Pl. IV.

Æ No.	Mint	Date	Weight and size	Obverse	Reverse
				COPPER	
351	—	(8)89	Wt. 210 S. ·7	As on No. 166.	As on No. 157.
351a	—	890	Wt. 216 S. ·7	As on No. 158, but date ٨٩٠	” *A.N.S. No. 77.*
351b	Mustafa-(bad)	(8)91	Wt. 216 S. ·7	” but date (٨)٩١	As on No. 153, but only top margin legible. *Mr. R. Antani's Collection.*
352	Mustafa-bad	892	Wt. 217 S. ·7	” but date ٨٩٢	As on No. 176, but top and left margins missing. Pl. IV.
353	—	(8)93	Wt. 217 S. ·7	” but date (٨)٩٣	As on No. 157.
354	—	893	Wt. 213 S. ·75	”	As on No. 333.
355	Mustafa-(bad)	”	Wt. 217 S. ·7	”	As on No. 318.
355a	—	(8)94	Wt. 218 S. ·65	As on No. 158, but date (٨)٩٤	As on No. 157. *Mr. R. Antani's Collection.*

Æ No.	Mint	Date	Weight and size	Obverse	Reverse
				COPPER	
355b	Mustafa-bad	895	Wt. 213 S. ·7	As on No. 158, but date ٨٩٥	As on No. 153, but bottom and left margins legible. *Mr. R. Antani's Collection.*
356	(Mustafa-) bad	896	Wt. 221 S. ·65	As on No. 167.	As on No. 303, but only left margin legible.
357	—	(8)96	Wt. 70 S. ·6	,,	As on No. 157.
358	—	897	Wt. 215 S. ·7	As on No. 168.	,,
359	—	898	Wt. 217 S. ·65	As on No. 169.	,,
360	— Shahr-i A'zam	899	Wt. 218 S. ·75	As on No. 158, but date ٨٩٩ in reverse form.	As on No. 176, but bottom and right margins missing.
361	—	900	Wt. 216 S. ·7	As on No. 171.	As on No. 157.
362	—	,,	Wt. 71 S. ·55	,,	,,

Æ No.	Mint	Date	Weight and size	Obverse	Reverse
				COPPER	
363	—	(9)01	Wt. 213 S. .75	As on No. 172.	Area as on No. 153, but defaced.
364		901	Wt. 147 S. ·65	As on No. 173.	As on No. 157.
365	—	(9)02	Wt. 220 S. ·7	As on No. 158, but date (٩)٠٢	As on No. 333.
366	—	902	Wt. 144 S. ·65	,,	As on No. 157.
367	—	,,	Wt. 69 S. ·55	,,	,,
368	—	904	Wt. 213 S. ·7	As on No. 174.	,,
369	—	(9)04	Wt. 145 S. ·6	,,	,,
370	—	,,	Wt. 71 S. ·5	,,	,,

Æ No.	Mint	Date	Weight and size	Obverse	Reverse
					COPPER
371	—	905	Wt. 217 S. ·75	As on No. 158, but date ۹۰۵	As on No. 157.
372	—	(9)05	Wt. 140 S. ·65	”	”
373	—	906	Wt. 214 S. ·75	As on No. 158, but date ۹۰۶	”
374	Mustafa-(bad.)	”	Wt. 140 S. ·6	”	As on No. 318. Pl. IV.
375	—	(9)06	Wt. 72 S. ·55	”	As on No. 157.
376	Mustafa-(bad) Shahr-i-A'zam.	907	Wt. 217 S. ·75	As on No. 175.	As on No. 311.
377	— Shahr-i-A'zam.	”	Wt. 67 S. ·65	”	As on No. 303, but top and left margins missing.
378	—	(9)07	Wt. 72 S. ·55	As on No. 175.	As on No. 157.

Æ No.	Mint	Date	Weight and size	Obverse	Reverse
				COPPER	
379	(Mustafa-bad) Shahr-i-A'zam.	(9)08	Wt. 218 S. ·7	As on No. 158, but date (٩)٠٨	As on No. 176, but right and bottom margins missing.
380	—	908	Wt. 72 S. ·55	,,	As on No. 157.
381	—	909	Wt. 220 S. ·7	As on No. 158, but date ٩٠٩	,,
382	—	(9)09	Wt. 140 S. ·65	,,	,,
383	—	,	Wt. 72 S. ·55	,,	,,
384	—	910	Wt. 215 S. ·7	As on No. 158, but date ٩١٠	,,
385	—	(9)10	Wt. 142 S. ·6	,,	,,
386	—	,,	Wt. 70 S. ·55	,,	,,

COPPER

Æ No.	Mint	Date	Weight and size	Obverse	Reverse
387	—	911	Wt. 215 S. ·75	As on No. 158, but date ٩١١ in reverse form.	As on No. 157.
388	—	,,	Wt. 209 S. ·65	,, but date ٩١١ with a cross X	,,
389	—	912	Wt. 219 S. ·7	,, but date ٩١٢	,,
390	—	(9)12	Wt. 169 S. ·65	,, but date (٩)١٢ in this form.	,,
391	Mustafa-(bad)	912	Wt. 139 S. ·65	As on No. 389.	Area as on No. 153, but right margin مصطفى
392	—	,,	Wt. 82 S. ·55	,,	As on No. 157.
393	—	,,	Wt. 71 S. ·55	,,	,,
393a	—	,,	Wt. 35·5 S. ·45	,,	,,

A.N.S. No. 92.

Æ No.	Mint	Date	Weight and size	Obverse	Reverse
				COPPER	
394	—	913	Wt. 219· S. ·65	As on No. 158, but date ٩١٣	As on No. 157.
395	—	(9)13	Wt. 170 S. ·65	,,	As on No. 189.
396	—	,,	Wt. 139 S. ·6	,,	As on No. 157.
397	—	(9)14	Wt. 206 S. ·7	As on No. 158, but date (٩)١٤	As on No. 333.
397a	—	,,	Wt. 70·5 S. ·55	,,	,, *A.N.S. No. 100.*
398	—	914	Wt. 218 S. ·7	As on No. 158, but date ٩١٤ in reverse form.	As on No. 157.
399	—	,,	Wt. 142· S. ·6	,,	,,
400	—	915	Wt. 216 S. ·7	As on No. 158, but date ٩١٥	,,

Æ No.	Mint	Date	Weight and size	Obverse	Reverse
					COPPER
401	—	(9)15	Wt. 70 S. ·55	As on No. 400.	As on No. 157.
402	—	916	Wt. 220 S. ·7	As on No. 158, but date ۹۱۶	,,
403	—	(9)16	Wt. 71 S. ·6	,,	,,
404	—	917	Wt. 219 S. ·7	As on No. 158, but date ۹۱۷	,,
405	—	(9)17	Wt. 145 S. ·65	,,	,,
406	—	919?	Wt. 214 S. ·7	As on No. 158, but date ۹۱۹ (?)	,,
407	—	(9)19(?)	Wt. 72 S. ·6	,,	,,
408	Muhamad-abad Shahr-i-Mukarram	905	Wt. 318 S. ·9	As on No. 187.	In curved diamond area السلطان شاه محمود *In Margins* :— ضرب شهر مکرم محمد آباد ۹۰۵ سنه Pl. IV.

Æ No.	Mint	Date	Weight and size	Obverse	Reverse
				COPPER	
409	—	—	Wt. 140 S. ·6	و ناصرالدنيا الفتح الدين ابو	In square السلطان محمود شاه Top margin خطر Pl. IV.
410	Ahmed-abad or Muhamad-abad	(9)10	Wt. 216 S. ·75	As on No. 385.	حمدآباد السلطان شاه شاه محمود بن محمد Pl. IV.
411	—	911	Wt. 213 S. ·7	As on No. 388, but without cross.	Area as on No. 248, but no margin. Pl. IV.
412	—	—	Wt. 219 S. ·75	As on No. 206.	As on No. 157.
413	—	—	Wt. 175 S. ·6	,,	As on No. 238, but no margin. Pl. IV.
414	—	—	Wt. 217 S. ·7	,,	In circle السلطان شاه محمود Pl. IV.
415	—	—	Wt. 141 S. ·6	,,	,,
416	—	—	Wt. 84 S. ·5	ناصر الدنيا	As on No. 157.

Æ No.	Mint	Date	Weight and size	Obverse	Reverse
				COPPER	
417	—	—	Wt. 14 S. ·35	^ دا ىب وا ا	As on No. 157.
418	Dîb ?	—	Wt. 34 S. ·4	As on No. 157.	,, but on one side ديب
419	—	—	Wt. 35 S. ·4	السلطان محمود شاه	As on No. 157.
420	—	—	Wt. 35 S. ·45	السلطان الاعظم الدنيا و	,,

MUZAFFAR SHĀH II.

Æ No.	Mint	Date	Weight and size	Obverse	Reverse
				GOLD	
AV 420a	—	920	Wt. 179 S. ·75	بد الرحمن المو بتائيد شمس و الدنيا الدين ابو النصر	السلطان محمود شاه بن مظفرشاه ٩٢٠ *B.M.C. Muh. States,* *No. 425.*
420b	—	,,	— S. ·8	In scalloped circle بد الرحمن المو بتائيد و شمس الدنيا الدين ابوالنصر	In scalloped circle السلطان شاه شاه مظفر بن محمود ٩٢٠ *B.M. No. 3.* (Recently acquired & not published) Pl. IV.
420c	—	924	Wt. 176 S. ·8	بد الرحمن المو بتائيد و شمس الدنيا الدين ابوالنصر	In scalloped circle السلطا شاه شاه مظفر بن محمود ٩٢٤ *I.M.C. No. 64.*

AV No.	Mint	Date	Weight and size	Obverse	Reverse
				GOLD	
420d	—	929	Wt. 177 S. ·75	As on No. 420a but differently arranged.	As on No. 420a but differently arranged and date ٩٢٩ *B. M. C. Muh. St. No. 426.*
420e	—	932	— S. ·8	In scalloped circle As on No. 420c.	In scalloped circle As on No. 420c but date ٩٣٢ over مظفر Pl. IV. *B. M. No. 9.* (*Recently acquired and not published.*)
				SILVER	
AR 421	—	920	Wt. 108 S. ·7	In dotted circle يد الرحمن المو بتائيد و شمس الدنيا الدين ابو النصر	In a square with peaked sides. السلطان شاه شاه ٩٢٠ مظفر محمود Margins illegible. Pl. IV.
422	—	,,	Wt. 110 S. ·65	,, but no dotted circle.	,,
423	—	,,	Wt. 110 S. ·7	,,	,, but in plain square.
424	—	921	Wt. 110 S. ·65	,,	,, but date ٩٢١

AR No.	Mint	Date	Weight and size	Obverse	Reverse
				SILVER	
424a	(Shahr-i-) Mukarram Muham- mad(abad)	921	Wt. 110 S. ·65	As on No. 422.	As on No. 424, but Right margin مكرم Top margin محمد *P. P. M. No. 20.*
425	—	922	Wt. 111 S. ·65	,,	As on No. 423, but date ٩٢٢
426	—	923	Wt. 110 S. ·65	,,	,, but date ٩٢٣
426a	(Shahr-i-) Mukarram Muham- mad(abad)	,,	Wt. 111 S. ·7	,,	,, but Right margin مكرم Top margin محمد *P. P. M. No. 21.*
427	—	925	Wt. 110 S. ·65	,,	As on No. 423, but date ٩٢٥
428	—	926	Wt. 108 S. ·65	,,	,, but date ٩٢٦
429	—	927	Wt. 110 S. ·65	,,	,, but date ٩٢٧
430	—	920	Wt. 110 S. ·7	يد الرحمن المو بتائيـــد شمـــس الدنيا و الدين ابو النصر	In circle السلطان محمود شاه بن مظفر شاه ٩٢٠

Æ No.	Mint	Date	Weight and size	Obverse	Reverse
					SILVER
431	—	925	Wt. 110 S. ·75	As on No. 430.	As on No. 430, but date ۹۲۵ Pl. IV.
432	—	,,	Wt. 95 S. ·7	,,	,,
433	—	926	Wt. 110 S. ·75	,,	,, but date ۹۲۶ and margin illegible
434	—	927	Wt. 110 S. ·7	,,	,, but date ۹۲۷
435	—	930	Wt. 109 S. ·7	,,	,, but date ۹۳۰
436	—	931	Wt. 110 S. ·65	,,	,, but date ۹۳۱
437	—	932	Wt. 108 S. ·75	,,	,, but date ۹۳۲
438	Mustafa-bad ?	—	Wt. 106 S. ·75	,,	As on No. 433, but no date and mint مصطفےاباد in the left margin. Pl. IV.

Æ No.	Mint	Date	Weight and size	Obverse	Reverse
				SILVER	
439	—	—	Wt. 54 S. ·6	As on No. 430.	As on No. 430, but no date.
440	Burhan-pur	921	Wt. 110 S. ·7	بتـأيـد المويد الرحمن شمـس و الدنيا الدين ابو النصر	In scalloped circle السلطان مظفر شاه في برهانپور ۹۲۱
440a	,,	?	Wt. 54·5 S. ·55	As on No. 422.	,, *A. N. S. No. 258.*
441	,,	922	Wt. 110 S. ·7	As on No. 440, but in dotted circle.	,, but date ۹۲۲ Pl. IV.
442	,,	923	Wt. 111 S. ·65	As on No. 430.	,, but date ۹۲۳
442a	,,	926	Wt. 110 S. ·7	As on No. 440.	,, but date ۹۲۶ *I. M. C. No. 51.*
443	,,	—	Wt. 111 S. ·7	يد ئيد المو بتا الرحمن و شمـس الدنيا الدين ابوالنصر	,, but date illegible.

SILVER

AR No.	Mint	Date	Weight and size	Obverse	Reverse
444	—	921	Wt. 78 S. ·55	شمس الدنيا و الدين ۹۲۱ ابو النصر	السلطان شاه شاه مظفر محمود
445	—	927	Wt. 172 S. ·65	,, but date ۹۲۷	,, Pl. IV.
446	Mustafa-bad Shahr-i-A'zam	926	Wt. 109 S. ·75	As on No. 421, but date ۹۲۶ in reverse form at the bottom.	In square with peaked sides. السلطان مظفر شاه خلد الله ملکه *Margins:*— Bottom شهر Right اعظم Top مصطفی Left باد Outer linear and dotted circle. Pl. IV.
447	—	92x	Wt. 111 S. ·7	As on No. 422.	In scalloped circle. السلطان مظفر شاه خلد الله ملکه Top right margins ۹۲ Pl. V.
448	—	—	Wt. 111 S. ·75	,,	In square with peaked sides. السلطان مظفر شاه الله خلد ملکه Pl. V.
448a	—	920	Wt. 110 S. ·7	,,	,, but date ۹۲۰ in right margin. *P. P. M. No. 24.*

AR No.	Mint	Date	Weight and size	Obverse	Reverse
				SILVER	
449	—	—	Wt. 110 S. ·75	As on No. 422.	As on No. 448 Pl. V.
450	—	—	Wt. 110 S. ·65	„	„
451	—	—	Wt. 107 S. ·7	„	„
452	—	—	Wt. 92 S. ·6	„	„
453	—	—	Wt. 52 S. ·5	„	„
454	—	—	Wt. 54 S. ·5	„	„ but not in peaked sided square.
455	—	926	Wt. 109 S. ·7	„	In square with peaked sides, within a circle السلطان شاه شاه ۹۲۶ مظفر محمود خلد الله ملکه
456	—	„	Wt. 55 S. ·55	„	„
457	—	929	Wt. 109 S. ·75	As on No. 421.	„ but date ۹۲۹

Æ No.	Mint	Date	Weight and size	Obverse	Reverse
				SILVER	
458	—	929	Wt. 104 S. ·7	As on No. 421.	As on No. 457.
459	—	92x	Wt. 53 S. ·55	As on No. 422.	” but date ٩٢x
460	—	930	Wt. 110 S. ·75	As on No. 421.	As on No. 455, but date ٩٣٠ in reverse form. Pl. V.
461	—	”	Wt. 106 S. ·7	”	” but within dotted circle.
461a	—	”	Wt. 55	”	As on No. 460. *I. M. C. No. 55.*
462	—	927	Wt. 110 S. ·75	As on No. 422.	In square with double sides peaked. Legend as on No. 421, but date ٩٢٧ Pl. V.
463	—	928	Wt. 111 S. ·7	”	” but date ٩٢٨
464	—	929	Wt. 110 S. ·8	”	” but date ٩٢٩

AR No.	Mint	Date	Weight and size	Obverse	Reverse
				SILVER	
465	—	930	Wt. 106 S. ·75	As on No. 422.	As on No. 462.
466	—	931	Wt. 111 S. ·75	,,	,, but date ٩٣١
467	—	932	Wt. 109 S. ·75	,,	,, but date ٩٣٢
468	—	929	Wt. 115 S. ·75	الرحمن بتائيد المويد شمس و الدنيا الدين ابو (النصر)	As on No. 464, but no double sided peaked square.
469	—	,,	Wt. 53 S. ·55	,,	,, Pl. V.
				COPPER	
Æ **470**	—	918	Wt. 215 S. ·65	As on No. 422, but date ٩١٨ in the centre.	As on No. 449, but no peaked sided square. Pl. V.
471	—	—	Wt. 216 S. ·7	As on No. 422.	,, but خلد ملكه written in 'Shikasta.' Pl. V.
472	—	—	Wt. 146 S. ·6	,,	As on No. 470.

Æ No.	Mint	Date	Weight and size	Obverse	Reverse
				COPPER	
473	—	—	Wt. 76 S. ·55	As on No. 422.	As on No. 470.
474	—	—	Wt. 69 S. ·5	,,	,, but lower portion missing.
475	—	918	Wt. 164 S. ·65	As on No. 444, but date ٩١٨	السلطان شاه مظفر
476	—	,,	Wt. 83 S. ·55	,,	,,
477	—	919	Wt. 164 S. ·7	,, but date ٩١٩	,,
478	—	920	Wt. 67 S. ·5	,, but date ٩٢٠	,,
478a	—	924	Wt. 86 S. ·6	,, but date ٩٢٤	,, *A. N. S. No. 104.*
479	—	920	Wt. 176 S. ·65	,, but date ٩٢٠	السلطان شاه شاه مظفر محمود Pl. V.

Æ No.	Mint	Date	Weight and size	Obverse	Reverse
					COPPER
480	—	922	Wt. 172 S. ·65	As on No. 444, but date ۹۲۲	As on No. 479.
480a	—	918	Wt. 217 S. ·7	المويد بتائيد الرحمن شمس الدنيا و الدين	In square السلطان شاه شاه ۹۱۸ محمود مظفر بن *I. M. C. No.* 57.
480b	—	924	Wt. 172 S. ·65	Illegible.	,, but date ۹۲۴, and in circle. *I. M. C. No. 59.*
481	—	,,	Wt. 128 S. ·65	As on No. 422.	In square السلطان شاه شاه ۹۲۴ مظفر بن محمود
482	—	9xx	Wt. 220 S. ·65	As on No. 468.	In scalloped circle ۹ مظفر بن محمود
483	—	,,	Wt. 84 S. ·5	As on No. 422.	As on No. 481, but date ۹xx
484	—	920	Wt. 176 S. ·7	الدنيا و الدين شمس ۹۲۰ ابو النصر	As on No. 430, but date on other side.
485	—	922	Wt. 163 S. ·7	,, but date ۹۲۲	,,

Æ No.	Mint	Date	Weight and size	Obverse	Reverse
				COPPER	
486	—	928	Wt. 169 S. ·7	As on No. 484.	As on No. 484.
486a	—	929	Wt. 173 S. ·75	,, but date ٩٢٩	,, *Gad. Coll.*
487	—	,,	Wt. 169 S. ·7	,, but figure ٢ of date ٩٢٩ in reverse form.	,, Pl. V.
488	—	930	Wt. 173 S. ·7	,, but date ٩٣٠	,,
488a	—	931	Wt. 167.5 S. ·7	,, but date ٩٣١	,, *A. N. S. No. 110.*
488b	—	,,	Wt. 85 S. ·6	,,	,, *Gad. Coll.*
489	—	932	Wt. 171 S. ·7	,, but date ٩٣٢	,,
489a	—	930	Wt. 262·5 S. ·8	As on No. 488.	,, but in square. *A. N. S. No. 115.*

Æ No.	Mint	Date	Weight and size	Obverse	Reverse
				COPPER	
489b	—	931	Wt. 263 S. ·75	As on No. 484, but date ۹۳۱	As on No. 489a. *Gad. Coll.*
490	—	932	Wt. 258 S. ·8	As on No. 489.	,, Pl. V.
490a	Burhan-pur	920	Wt. 166 S. ·7	As on No. 484.	السلطان شاه مظـــفر برهانپور *Gad. Coll.*
490b	,,	921	Wt. 165 S. ·7	,, but date ۹۲۱	السلطان شاه مظـــفر سـعـد شهرهالی *Gad. Coll.*
491	,,	922	Wt. 166 S. ·7	As on No. 485.	السلطان شــــاه مظـــفر Lower portion probably the mint, is illegible. Pl. V.
492	,,	923	Wt. 168 S. ·8	As on No. 484, but date ۹۲۳	,,
492a	,,	,,	Wt. 171 S. ·7	,,	In circle السلطان شاه مظفر Right side margin برهانپور *Gad. Coll.*
492b	—	922	Wt. 166 S. ·7	,, but date ۹۲۲	As on No. 493, below. *Gad. Coll.*

Æ No.	Mint	Date	Weight and size	Obverse	Reverse
				COPPER	
493	—	924	Wt. 167 S. ·7	As on No. 484, but date ٩٢٤	In circle السلطان ه محمـــود شا مظفر بن شـــاه Pl. V.
494	—	925	Wt. 169 S. ·75	" but date ٩٢٥	"
495	—	"	Wt. 151 S. ·7	"	"
495a	—	(9)25	Wt. 85 S. ·6	"	" *Gad. Coll.*
496	—	926	Wt. 168 S. ·75	" but date ٩٢٦	"
496a	—	—	Wt. 162 S. ·75	As on No. 422.	" *Gad. Coll.*
497	—	926	Wt. 219 S. ·7	"	السلطان مظفر ٩٢٦ شاه خلد الله
498	—	928	Wt. 215 S. ·7	"	" but date ٩٢٨

Æ No.	Mint	Date	Weight and size	Obverse	Reverse
				COPPER	
499	—	928	Wt. 143 S. ·6	As on No. 422.	As on No. 498.
500	—	929	Wt. 220 S. ·65	,,	As on No. 497 but date ۹۲۹
501	—	92x	Wt. 146 S. ·6	,,	,, but date ۹۲x
502	—	930	Wt. 220 S. ·7	,,	,, but date ۹۳۰ in reverse form Pl. V.
503	—	9xx	Wt. 72 S. ·55	,,	(السلطان) مظفر ۹ شاه
504	—	,,	Wt. 34 S. ·45	,,	السلطان مظفر ۹ شاه Pl. V.
505	—	,,	Wt. 16 S. ·35	,,	,,
506	—	921	Wt. 222 S. ·7	الدینا شمس ۹۲۱ وبت الدابوالنصر	In square السلطان شاه مظفر

Æ No.	Mint	Date	Weight and size	Obverse	Reverse
				COPPER	
506a	—	923	Wt. 170 S. ·7	As on No. 484, but date ۹۲۳	In circle السلطان شاه مظفر *W. M. R.*
506b	—	929	Wt. 216 S. ·7	As on 507 below but date ۹۲۹ at bottom.	As on No. 507 below. *W. M. R.*
507	—	—	Wt. 214 S. ·65	و الدنيا شمس ابوالنصر الدين ۹	In square السلطان شاه مظفر
508	—	927	Wt. 173 S. ·6	As on No. 422.	السلطان ۹۲۷ شاه مظفر
509	—	9xx	Wt. 36 S. ·4	,,	,,
510	—	929	Wt. 143 S. ·6	As on No. 444, but date ۹۲۹	As on No. 507.
511	—	,,	Wt. 70 S. ·5	,,	,,
512	—	930	Wt. 170 S. ·6	,, but date ۹۳۰	السلطان شاه مظفر Bottom margin شهر

MAHMŪD SHĀH II ?

Æ No.	Mint	Date	Weight and size	Obverse	Reverse
				COPPER	
513	—	—	Wt. 140 S. ·6	ناصر الدنيا والدين ابو الفتح	ناصر شاه السلطان Pl. V.
514	—	—	Wt. 134 S. ·6	,,	,,
515	—	—	Wt. 134 S. ·65	,,	,,
516	—	—	Wt. 65 S. ·5	,,	,, Pl. V.

BAHADŪR SHĀH.

AR No.	Mint	Date	Weight and size	Obverse	Reverse
				SILVER	
517	—	933	Wt. 129 S. ·8	قطب الدنيا والدين ابو الفضل بهادر شاه بن مظفر شاه M. M. ♈	بن محمود شاه بن محمد شاه بن احمد شاه بن محمد شاه بن مظفر شاه ٩٣٣ Pl. V.
518	—	941	Wt. 33 S. ·55	In scalloped circle بهادر شاه M. M. ♈	In scalloped circle السلطان ٩٤١ سنه

Æ No.	Mint	Date	Weight and size	Obverse	Reverse
				SILVER	
519	—	941	Wt. 35 S. ·5	As on No. 518, but in dotted circle.	As on No. 518, but in dotted circle. Pl. V.
520	—	,,	Wt. 34 S. ·5	,,	,,
521	—	943	Wt. 32 S. ·45	,, but in plain circle.	,, but in plain circle and date ۹۴۳
522	—	,,	Wt. 16 S. ·35	As on No. 519, but no M. M.	As on No. 519, but date ۹۴۳
522a	—	,,	Wt. 35 S. ·5	In double six foil السلطان العادل ۹۴۳	In double six foil شاه بهادر مظفر شاه بن Pl. V. *N. C. 5th Ser. Vol. IV, p. 104.*
523	—	942	Wt. 110 S. ·7	الرحمن المويد بتائيد ناصر الدنيا و الدين ابوالنصر	السلطان شاه شاه بهادر بن ۹۴۳ مظفر *M. M. X.* Pl. VI.
524	—	943	Wt. 106 S. ·7	,, but in place of ناصر, شمس	,, but in peaked sided square and date ۹۴۳
525	—	—	Wt. 111 S. ·7	قطب الدنيا و الدين ابوالفضل M. M. ф Date at the bottom illegible.	In circle السلطان مظفر شاه بن بهادر شاه Pl. VI.

Æ No.	Mint	Date	Weight and size	Obverse	Reverse
				COPPER	
526	—	932	Wt. 220 S. ·65	السلطان بهادر شاه	اثنتي (و ثلثين) سنه تسعمايه ٩٣٢
527	—	,,	Wt. 145 S. ·6	,,	,, Pl. VI.
528	—	9X2	Wt. 71 S. ·5	,,	,,
529	—	933	Wt. 220 S. ·65	,,	,, but date ٩٣٣ Pl. VI.
530	—	,,	Wt. 146 S. ·6	,,	,,
531	—	934	Wt. 219 S. ·65	,,	As on No. 526, but date ٩٣٤
532	—	(9)34	Wt. 219 S. ·65	ابو الفضل قطب الدنيا و الدين	السلطان مظفر بن بهادر شاه شاه (٩)٣٤
533	—	93x	Wt. 218 S. ·65	,,	,, but date ٩٣x

COPPER

Æ No.	Mint	Date	Weight and size	Obverse	Reverse
534	—	93x	Wt. 218 S. ·6	السلطان ابو المظفر قطب الدينا والدين	As on No. 533. Pl. VI.
535	—	—	Wt. 145 S. ·55	As on No. 532.	As on No. 532, but no date.
536	—	—	Wt. 72 S. ·5	,,	,,
537	—	934	Wt. 171 S. ·7	As on No. 525, but date ۹۳۴ in centre and no M. M.	As on No. 525. Pl. VI.
538	—	935	Wt. 168 S. ·65	,, but date ۹۳۵	,,
539	—	,,	Wt. 77 S. ·6	,,	,,
540	—	,,	Wt. 86 S. ·55	,, but figure 5 of date 935 inscribed like this ﻻ	,, Pl. VI.
540a	—	937	Wt. 168 S. ·7	As on No. 537, but date ۹۳۷	,, *Gad. Coll.*

Æ No.	Mint	Date	Weight and size	Obverse	Reverse
				COPPER	
541	—	938	Wt. 172 S. ·65	As on No. 537, but date ٩٣٨	As on No. 525.
542	—	939	Wt. 169 S. ·65	,, but date ٩٣٩	,,
543	—	(9)42	Wt. 176 S. ·7	,, but date (٩) ٤٢	,,
544	—	943	Wt. 169 S. ·65	,, but date ٩٤٣	,,
545	—	93x	Wt. 263 S. ·75	,, but date ٩٣x	As on No. 537, but in square. Pl. VI.
545a	—	935	Wt. 251 S. ·75	,, but date ٩٣٥	,, *A. N. S. No. 117.*
545b	—	937	Wt. 262 S. ·75	,, but date ٩٣٧	,, *Gad. Coll.*
545c	—	938	Wt. 264 S. ·75	As on No. 541.	,, *Gad. Coll.*

Æ No.	Mint	Date	Weight and size	Obverse	Reverse
				COPPER	
545d	—	938	Wt. 131 S. ·6	As on No. 541.	As on No. 545. *Gad. Coll.*
546	—	939	Wt. 130 S. ·7	As on No. 542.	,,
546a	—	940	Wt. 253 S. ·75	As on No. 537, but date ٩٤٠	As on No. 525. *I. M. C. No. 66.*
546b	—	942	Wt. 259 S. ·75	As on No. 543.	As on No. 545. *Gad. Coll.*
547	—	943	Wt. 257 S. ·75	As on No. 544.	,,
548	—	937	Wt. 216 S. ·7	As on No. 537, but date ٩٣٧	بهادر شاه بنمظفر شاه السلطان Pl. VI.
549	—	,,	Wt. 212 S. ·7	,,	,,
550	—	,,	Wt. 211 S. ·7	,,	,, but in peaked sided square.

Æ No.	Mint	Date	Weight and size	Obverse	Reverse
				COPPER	
50a	—	937	Wt. 142 S. ·6	As on No. 548.	As on No. 550. *A. N. S. No. 121.*
551	—	938	Wt. 213 S. ·75	As on No. 541.	As on No. 548.
552	—	939	Wt. 216 S. ·75	As on No. 542.	,,
553	—	,,	Wt. 141 S. ·75	,, but in circle.	As on No. 550.
554	—	xx0	Wt. 217 S. ·75	As on No. 537, but date xx.	As on No. 548, but in circle. Pl. VI.
555	—	938	Wt. 216 S. ·7	As on No. 525, but date ٩٣٨ in bottom and No M. M.	As on No. 548
556	—	93x	Wt. 144 S. ·7	,, but date ٩٣x and in circle.	,, Pl. VI.
556a	—	938	Wt. 95 S. ·6	٩٣٨ الدنيا قطب والدين	,, *I. M. C. No. 74.*

Æ No.	Mint	Date	Weight and size	Obverse	Reverse
				COPPER	
557	—	938	Wt. 218 S. ·8	As on No. 555.	As on No. 548. Pl. VI.
558	—	,,	Wt. 215 S. ·75	,,	بن بهادر شاه ن السلطا Pl. VI.
559	—	—	Wt. 48 S. ·6	والدنيا قطب الدين	بهادر شاه مظفر شاه Pl. VI.
560	—	(9)43	Wt. 86 S. ·55	As on No. 544.	السلطان بن مظفر بهادر شاه
561	—	943	Wt. 82 S. ·6	,,	,, Pl. VI.
562	—	938	Wt. 219 S. ·7	As on No. 541, but in circle.	بهادر شاه بن مظفر السلطان Pl. VI.
562a	—	,,	Wt. 220·5 S. ·75	,,	,, but in a scalloped circle. *A. N. S. No. 123.*
563	—	(9)38	Wt. 207 S. ·8	As on No. 541.	,,

Æ No.	Mint	Date	Weight and size	Obverse	Reverse
					COPPER
564	—	938	Wt. 139 S. ·7	As on No. 562.	As on No. 562.
565	—	,,	Wt. 134 S. ·6	,,	,,
566	—	(9)38	Wt. 126 S. ·7	As on No. 563.	,,
567	—	938	Wt. 69 S. ·6	As on No. 541.	,,
568	—	(9)38	Wt. 53 S. ·65	As on No. 563.	,,
569	—	942	Wt. 221 S. ·65	As on No. 537, but date ۹۴۲	شاه بهادر مظفر شاه السلطان Pl. VI.
570	—	,,	Wt. 145 S. ·6	,,	,,
571	—	—	Wt. 215 S. ·65	قطب الدنيا الدين و ابوالفضل	شاه بهادر مظفر شاه

Æ No.	Mint	Date	Weight and size	Obverse	Reverse
					COPPER
572	—	—	Wt. 140 S. ·6	As on No. 571.	As on No. 571.
573	—	—	Wt. 72 S. ·5	,,	,,
574	—	—	Wt. 56 S. ·6	Illegible.	بهادر شاه Pl. VI.
575	—	—	Wt. 59 S. ·5	والدين قطب الدنيا	بهادر شاه السلطان
576	—	934?	Wt. 219 S. ·65	Reverse As on No. 531.	As on No. 533.
577	—	—	Wt. 144 S. ·6	,, but no date	,,
578	—	—	Wt. 218 S. ·65	As on No. 526.	Obverse As on No. 534.
578a	—	941	Wt. 70·5 S. ·5	As on No. 537, but date ٩٤١	بهادر شاه مظفر شاه *I. M. C. No. 75.*

SHAH-I-HIND SERIES.
VARIETY NO. 1.

Æ No.	Mint	Date	Weight and size	Obverse	Reverse
				COPPER	
579	— (Shahr-i-) Mukar- ram.	(9)35	Wt. 129 S. ·6	هر کرا روی ورواجی بوسطح زمین هست M. M. ♈ over س of سطح	In square سکه اقبال هند (۹)۳ع ده دارد برجبین Right margin مُکرّم
580	—	935	Wt. 62 S. ·5	,,	,, but no margin.
581	—	936	Wt. 130 S. ·6	,,	,, but date ۹۳۶ and no margin.
582	— Shahr-i- (Mukar- ram.)	937	Wt. 131 S. ·6	,,	,, but date ۹۳۷ and bottom margin شهر Pl. VI.
583	— (Shahr-i-) Mukar- ram.	(9)37	Wt. 131 S. ·6	,,	,, but right margin مُکرّم
584	Muham- mad(abad)	937	Wt. 131 S. ·6	,,	,, but top margin محمّد Pl. VII.
585	Muham- mad?(abad)	,,	Wt. 64 S. ·5	,,	,,

Æ No.	Mint	Date	Weight and size	Obverse	Reverse
				COPPER	
586	— (Shahr-i-) Mukar-ram	(9)38	Wt. 131 S. ·6	As on No. 579.	As on No. 579, but date (٩)٣٨ Pl. VII.
587	Muham-mad(abad)	938	Wt. 131 S. ·6	,,	As on No. 584, but date ٩٣٨
588	— (Shahr-i-) Mukar-ram	,,	Wt. 66 S. ·5	,,	As on No. 586.
589	— Shahr-i-(Mukar-ram)	939	Wt. 133 S. ·6	,,	As on No. 582, but date ٩٣٩
590	Muham-mad(abad)	,,	Wt. 132 S. ·55	,,	As on No. 584, but date ٩٣٩
591	,,	,,	Wt. 66 S. ·5	,,	,,
592	— Shahr-i-(Mukar-ram)	940	Wt. 129 S. ·6	,,	As on No. 582, but date ٩٤٠
593	,,	,,	Wt. 66 S. ·5	,,	,,

Æ No.	Mint	Date	Weight and size	Obverse	Reverse
				COPPER	
594	Muham-mad(abad)	—	Wt. 130 S. ·65	As on No. 579.	As on No. 584, but no date. Pl. VII.
				VARIETY NO. 2.	
595	—	938	Wt. 130 S. ·65	هر كرا روے هست و رواجى سطح برزمين	In dotted circle سكۀ اقبال ٩٣٨ ه هند دارد برجبين
596	—	(9)38	Wt. 67 S. ·5	,,	,, but no circle.
597	—	938	Wt. 31 S. ·45	,,	,,
598	—	939	Wt. 132 S. ·6	,,	,, but date ٩٣٩ Pl. VII.
599	—	,,	Wt. 64 S. ·45	,,	,,

MAHMŪD SHĀH III.

Æ No.	Mint	Date	Weight and size	Obverse	Reverse
				GOLD	
AV **599a**	—	946	Wt. 185 S. ·8	الواثق المنان بالله الفتح الدنيا والدين ابو ناصر	Within double square. السلطان شاه شاه محمود بن لطيف In lowest segment ٩٤٦ *B. M. C. No. 428*

AV No.	Mint	Date	Weight and size	Obverse	Reverse
					GOLD
599b	—	947	Wt. 185 S. ·8	As on No. 599a.	As on No. 599a, but date ٩٤٧ *B. M. C. No. 429.*
599c	—	949	Wt. 185 S. ·75	,,	,, but date ٩٤٩ *B. M. C. No. 430.*
599d	—	950	Wt. 185 S. ·8	,,	,, but date ٩٤٠ above محمود *B. M. C. No. 431.*
599e	—	956	Wt. 185 S. ·75	,,	,, but date ٩٥٦ *B. M. C. No. 432.*
599f	—	960	Wt. 185 S. ·8	,,	As on No. 599d, but date ٩٦٠ *B. M. C. No. 433.*
					SILVER
AR **600**	—	950	Wt. 110 S. ·7	**As on No. 599a.**	In double square with peaked sides. السلطان شاه شاه محمود ٩٤٠ بن لطيف
601	—	,,	Wt. 110 S. ·7	,,	,, Pl. VII.

AR. No.	Mint	Date	Weight and size	Obverse	Reverse
				SILVER	
602	—	950	Wt. 109 S. ·7	As on No. 599a.	As on No. 600.
603	—	951	Wt. 108 S. ·7	,,	,, but date ٩٥١
604	—	952	Wt. 110 S. ·7	,,	,, but date ٩٥٢
605	—	959	Wt. 108 S. ·8	,,	,, but date ٩٥٩
606	—	95x	Wt. 55 S. ·5	,,	,, but date ٩٥x
607	—	951	Wt. 110 S. ·7	الدنيا والدين ابو ناصر الفتح المنان الواثق بالله ٩٥١	In circle السلطان لطيف شاه بن محمود شاه Pl. VII.
608	—	961	Wt. 110 S. ·65	,, but date ٩٦١	,,
609	—	,,	Wt. 101 S. ·65	,,	,,

Æ No.	Mint	Date	Weight and size	Obverse	Reverse
				SILVER	
610	—	961	Wt. 53 S. ·5	As on No. 608.	As on No. 607.
611	—	(9)61	Wt. 35 S. ·5	,, but date (٩)٦١	,,
612	—	—	Wt. 53 S. ·6	As on No. 607, but no date.	,,
613	—	955	Wt. 115 S. ·7	As on No. 600.	As on No. 600, but in scalloped circle and date ٩٥٥ above لطيف
614	—	957	Wt. 112 S. ·7	,,	,, but date ٩٥٧
615	—	958	Wt. 115 S. ·65	,,	,, but date ٩٥٨
616	—	960	Wt. 132 S. ·75	,,	,, but date ٩٦٠ Pl. VII.
617	—	,,	Wt. 129 S. ·8	,,	,,

SILVER

AR No.	Mint	Date	Weight and size	Obverse	Reverse
618	—	(9)60	Wt. 65 S. ·6	As on No. 600.	As on No. 616, but no scalloped circle.
618a	—	961	Wt. 132·5 S. ·8	,,	,, but date ٩٦١ *A. N. S. No. 259.*
619	—	955	Wt. 117 S. ·7	,,	As on No. 613, but in double square with peaked sides.
620	—	,,	Wt. 57 S. ·55	,,	,,
621	—	956	Wt. 117 S. ·7	,,	,, but date ٩٥٦
622	—	957	Wt. 111 S. ·7	,,	,, but date ٩٥٧
623	—	(9)57	Wt. 56 S. ·6	,,	,,
624	—	958	Wt. 116 S. ·7	,,	As on No. 619, but date ٩٥٨

AR No.	Mint	Date	Weight and size	Obverse	Reverse
				SILVER	
625	—	958	Wt. 56 S. ·6	As on No. 600.	As on No. 624.
626	—	,,	Wt. 111 S. ·7	,,	As on No. 600, but date ٩٥٨ in بن
627	—	,,	Wt. 101 S. ·7	,,	,,
628	Ahmed?-(abad)	959	Wt. 111 S. ·7	,,	,, but date ٩٥٩. Bottom margin احمد Pl. VII.
629	—	,,	Wt. 105 S. ·75	,,	,, but no margin.
				COPPER	
Æ 630	Muhammadabad Shahr-i-(Mukarram)	944	Wt. 240 S. ·7	In square الدين صرو ناالدنيا *Margins*— Bottom شهر Right illegible. Top محمد Left آباد	In square السلطان محمود شاه Bottom margin ٩٤٤ Pl. VII.
630a	—	(9)44	Wt. 172 S. ·65	ناالدنيا و صر الدين (٩)٤٤	In double circle السلطان محمود شاه *A. N. S. No. 154.*

Æ No.	Mint	Date	Weight and size	Obverse	Reverse
				COPPER	
631	—	945	Wt. 146 S. ·65	الدنیا ناصر والدین ابو الفتح	In circle السلطان لطیف شاه محمود بن Bottom margin ۹۴ع Pl. VII.
632	—	—	Wt. 148 S. ·65	,, but in circle and M. M. ⸸	,, but no date.
633	—	—	Wt. 146 S. ·65	,, but No. M. M.	,, Pl. VII.
634	—	xx5	Wt. 140 S. ·65	As on No. 631, but figure ع on right bottom.	,,
635	—	948	Wt. 131 S. ·6	والدین الدنیا ۹۴۸ ناصر ابو الفتح	In circle السلطان شاه شاه لطیف محمود بن
636	—	949	Wt. 140 S. ·65	الدنیا ناصر والدین ۹۴۹ ابو الفتح	As on No. 632.
637	—	(9)49	Wt. 73 S. ·55	,, but date (۹)۴۹	As on No. 631, but no date.
638	—	—	Wt. 73 S. ·55	As on No. 631.	As on No. 632.

Æ No.	Mint	Date	Weight and size	Obverse	Reverse
					COPPER
639	—	—	Wt. 75 S. ·6	As on No. 600.	السلطان شاه لطيف بن محمود
640	—	—	Wt. 35 S. ·45	,,	,,
640a	—	944	Wt. 221·5 S. ·65	In square الدين ٩٤٤ ناصر و الدنيا	In square السلطان محمود شاه *A. N. S. No. 156.*
641	—	945	Wt. 69 S. ·55	,, but date ٩٤٥	,,
642	—	946	Wt. 216 S. ·75	,, but date ٩٤٦	,, Pl. VII.
643	—	(9)46?	Wt. 198 S. ·7	,, but date illegible.	,,
644	—	—	Wt. 141 S. ·6	As on No. 641, but no date.	,,

Æ No.	Mint	Date	Weight and size	Obverse	Reverse
					COPPER
645	—	—	Wt. 72 S. ·55	As on No. 644.	As on No. 641. Pl. VII.
646	—	—	Wt. 219 S. ·7	,,	,,
647	—	—	Wt. 212 S. ·7	,,	In square السلطان محمود شاه
648	—	—	Wt. 146 S. ·65	,,	,,
649	—	—	Wt. 138 S. ·6	,,	As on No. 641.
649a	—	(9)59	Wt. 142 S. ·65	,,	In square with peaked sides السلطان شاه محمود ٩ع(٩) *A. N. S. No. 162.*
650	—	948	Wt. 138 S. ·65	الدنيا ٩٤٨ و ناصــــر الدين ابوالفتح	As on No. 635.
651	—	949	Wt. 69 S. ·5	As on No. 635, but date ٩٤٩ and both ٩ in reverse form.	,,

Æ No.	Mint	Date	Weight and size	Obverse	Reverse
				COPPER	
652	—	951	Wt. 148 S. ·65	الدنيا ٩٤١ ناصر والدين ابو الفتح Figure ٤ like ٣	As on No. 635.
653	—	959	Wt. 140 S. ·6	,, but date ٩٣٢	,, Pl. VII.
654	—	x49	Wt. 146 S. ·6	As on No. 600, but date x٤٩ above الفتح	As on No. 600, but in circle and no date.
655	—	949	Wt. 70 S. ·55	,,	,, Pl. VII.
656	—	,,	Wt. 147 S. ·6	As on No. 631.	As on No. 631, but date ٩٤٩ in بن
657	—	,,	Wt. 144 S. ·6	الدنيا ناصر والدين ابوالفتح	السلطان ٩٤٩ شاه لطيف محمود بن
658	—	950	Wt. 140 S. ·6	In circle ناصر الدنيا والدين	In square السلطان شاه شاه ٩٥٠ محمود لطيف (מה)מוד. Pl. VII.
659	—	951	Wt. 144 S. ·6	و الدنيا ناصر الدين ٩٤١ ابوالفتح	In square السلطان شاه محمود Bottom margin ٩٤١ Pl. VII.

Æ No.	Mint	Date	Weight and size	Obverse	Reverse
					COPPER
660	—	951	Wt. 32 S. ·45	المتان الواثق	السلطان شاه شاه ۹۵۱
661	—	953	Wt. 219 S. ·7	As on No. 600.	As on No. 600, but not in peaked sided square and date ۹۵۳
662	—	,,	Wt. 72 S. ·55	,,	,,
663	—	952	Wt. 214 S. ·65	الدنيا ناصر الفتح والدين ابو	السلطان شاه لطيف ۹۵۲ محمود x over Mahmud. Pl. VII.
664	—	956	Wt. 142 S. ·65	As on No. 600.	,, but date ۹۵۶ and no cross.
665	—	,,	Wt. 67 S. ·5	,,	,, Pl. VIII.
665a	Shahr-i-Mu'azzam	953	Wt. 221·5 S. ·7	الدنيا ناصر والدين ۹۵۳	In square شاه محمود Left margin شهر Top معظم *A. N. S. No. 136.*

Æ No.	Mint	Date	Weight and size	Obverse	Reverse
				COPPER	
665b	—	953	Wt. 68 S. ·5	As no No. 665a.	As on No. 665a, but no margin. *W. M. R.*
666	(Ahmed-) ābād	954	Wt. 216 S. ·75	الدنيا ناصر والدين ٩٥٤	In square شاه محمود Right margin آباد
667	(Ahmed-) ābād	,,	Wt. 210 S. ·7	,,	,,
668	Ahmed- (ābād) (Shahr-i-) Mu'azzam	,,	Wt. 146 S. ·6	,,	,, but Left margin معظم Top ,, احمد
669	—	,,	Wt. 69 S. ·55	,,	,, but no margin.
669a	—	,,	Wt. 219 S. ·7	,,	السلطان شاه شاه محمود بن لطيف ٩٥٤ *A. N. S. No. 169.*
670	— Shahr-i- (Mu'azzam)	(9)55	Wt. 144 S. ·6	,, but date (٩)٥٥	As on No. 666, but right margin شهر Pl. VIII.
671	(Ahmed- ābād) Shahr-i- Mu'azzam	955	Wt. 142 S. ·6	,,	,, but Left margin شهر Top معظم Pl. VIII.

COPPER

Æ No.	Mint	Date	Weight and size	Obverse	Reverse
672	Ahmed-ābād	956	Wt. 211 S. ·75	As on No. 666, but date ٩٥٦	As on No. 666, but Top margin احمد Right „ آباد Pl. VIII.
673	Ahmed-ābād.	„	Wt. 140 S. ·6	„	„
674	—	xx6	Wt. 69 S. ·55	As on No. 666, but date xx٦	As on No. 669.
675	— Shahr-i-(Mu'az-zam.)	(9)57	Wt. 143 S. ·7	„ but date (٩)٥٧	As on No. 666, but Bottom margin شهر
676	—	„	Wt. 131 S. ·6	„	As on No. 669.
676a	—	957	Wt. 71 S. ·55	„	„ *O. No. 24.*
677	—	958	Wt. 200 S. ·65	As on No. 666, but date ٩٥٨	„
678	—	„	Wt. 66 S. ·55	„	„

COPPER

Æ No.	Mint	Date	Weight and size	Obverse	Reverse
678a	Ahmed-ābād	960	Wt. 219 S. ·7	As on No. 666, but date ٩٦٠	As on No. 672. *B. B. R. A. S.*
679	—	(9)60	Wt. 142 S. ·65	”	As on No. 669.
680	—	(9)56	Wt. 222 S. ·7	As on No. 600.	As on No. 613, but date (٩)٥٦
681	—	”	Wt. 210 S. ·7	”	” Pl. VIII.
682	—	956	Wt. 146 S. ·5	”	”
683	—	(9)56	Wt. 142 S. ·75	”	” Pl. VIII.
684	—	xx6	Wt. 144 S. ·7	”	”
685	—	(9)57	Wt. 69 S. ·55	”	As on No. 614.

Æ No.	Mint	Date	Weight and size	Obverse	Reverse
					COPPER
686	—	(9)59	Wt. 66 S. ·55	As on No. 600.	As on No. 613, but date (٩)ع٩ in reverse form.
687	—	95x	Wt. 67 S. ·5	Illegible, but date ٩عx at the top	,, but no date. Pl. VIII.
688	—	959	Wt. 216 S. ·7	As on No. 600.	,, but in plain circle and date ٩ع٩
689	—	xx0	Wt. 219 S. ·7	,,	As on No. 618, but date xx•
690	—	960	Wt. 171 S. ·65	المفا لواثق با	As on No. 618.
691	—	,,	Wt. 168 S. ·7	As on No. 600.	,,
692	—	(9)60	Wt. 87 S. ·5	,,	,,
693	—	956	Wt. 219 S. ·65	As on No. 664.	As on No. 682, but in hexagon. Pl. VIII.

Æ No.	Mint	Date	Weight and size	Obverse	Reverse
				COPPER	
694	—	xx6	Wt. 215 S. ·7	As on No. 674.	As on No. 635, but no circle.
695	—	xx7	Wt. 218 S. ·65	As on No. 675.	,,
696	—	957	Wt. 147 S. ·7	As on No. 676.	,, but in square. Pl. VIII.
696a	—	958	Wt. 218 S. ·7	As on No. 677.	,, but top margin خطهٔ *Gad. Coll.*
697	—	—	Wt. 141 S. ·65	As on No. 666, but no date.	As on No. 694.
698	—	958	Wt. 218 S. ·65	الدنيا الفـــــــتح ٩٤٨ والدين ابو	As on No. 618, but no date.
699	—	—	Wt. 140 S. ·6	As on No. 600.	As on No. 655.
700	—	—	Wt. 37 S. ·45	,,	,,

Æ No.	Mint	Date	Weight and size	Obverse	Reverse
				COPPER	
701	—	—	Wt. 34 S. ·4	As on No. 600.	As on No. 655.
702	—	—	Wt. 143 S. ·6	,,	As on No. 654.
703	—	—	Wt. 66 S. ·5	,,	,,
704	Daulatābād ?	—	Wt. 145 S. ·6	,,	,, mint Daulatābād in the top margin. Pl. VIII.
705	?	—	Wt. 68 S. ·5	,,	,, but margin illegible Pl. VIII.
706	— Shahr-i-	—	Wt. 65 S. ·55	,,	,, in margin, شهر Pl. VIII.
707	—	957	Wt. 218 S. ·7	As on No. 676.	As on No. 676.
708	—	,,	Wt. 216 S. ·65	Legend illegible M. M. 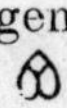 and date ٩٤٧	As on No. 647. Pl. VIII.

Æ No.	Mint	Date	Weight and size	Obverse	Reverse
				COPPER	
709	—	—	Wt. 146 S. ·6	As on No. 708.	As on No. 647.
710	—	958	Wt. 218 S. ·7	As on No. 698.	As on No. 643.
711	—	—	Wt. 212 S. ·7	In circle الدّنيا ناصر و الدين * in centre	As on No. 647. Pl. VIII.
711a	—	961	Wt. 260 S. ·85	As on No. 607 but date ٩٢١ or ٩٦١	As on No. 607, but in square. Pl. VIII. *B. B. R. A. S.*
712	—	—	Wt. 130 S. ·6	,, but no date.	,,
713	—	961	Wt. 173 S. ·7	As on No. 711a.	As on No. 607.
714	—	—	Wt. 164 S. ·7	As on No. 712.	,,
715	—	—	Wt. 88 S. ·65	,,	,,

Æ No.	Mint	Date	Weight and size	Obverse	Reverse
				COPPER	
715a	—	961	Wt. 46 S. ·5	As on No. 711a.	As on No. 607. *I. M. C. No. 96.*
716	—	—	Wt. 166 S. ·65	As on No. 712.	,, margin illegible.
717	—	—	Wt. 71 S. ·5	Illegible.	السلطان شا محمود Pl. VIII.
				AHMAD SHAH, III.	
				GOLD	
AV 717a	—	962	Wt. 91·5 S. ·6	المعتصم المحامد و الدنيا الدين غياث	السلطان شاه شاه عمر ٩٦٢ احمد بن محمود Pl. VIII. *P. M. L. No. 6934.*
				SILVER	
AR 718	—	961	Wt. 167 S. ·9	In circle الرحمن بالله المعتصم المحامد و الدنيا الدين ابو غياث	In double square with peaked sides. السلطان شاه شاه عمر ٩٦١ احمد بن محمود Pl. VIII.
719	—	962	Wt. 166 S. ·85	,,	,, but date ٩٦٢
720	—	,,	Wt. 167 S. ·8	,,	,,

Æ No.	Mint	Date	Weight and size	Obverse	Reverse
					SILVER
721	—	962	Wt. 137 S. ·8	As on No. 718.	As on No. 719.
722	—	,,	Wt. 107 S. ·7	,,	,,
723	—	,,	Wt. 82 S. ·65	,,	,,
724	—	963	Wt. 222 S. ·85	,,	As on No. 718 but date ٩٦٣ Pl. VIII.
725	—	,,	Wt. 109 S. ·7	,,	,,
725a	—	964	—	,,	,, *W. M. R.*
726	—	965	Wt. 221 S. ·8	,,	As on No. 718, but date ٩٦٥
727	—	,,	Wt. 111 S. ·65	,,	,,

Æ No.	Mint	Date	Weight and size	Obverse	Reverse
				SILVER	
728	—	965	Wt. 54 S. ·55	As on No. 718.	As on No. 726.
729	—	966	Wt. 104 S. ·7	,,	As on No. 718, but date ٩٦٦
730	—	967	Wt. 110 S. ·7	,,	,, but date ٩٦٧
731	—	968	Wt. 110 S. ·65	,,	,, but date ٩٦٨
732	—	,,	Wt. 53 S. ·55	,,	,,
				COPPER	
Æ 732a	—	961	Wt. 223 S. ·7	In circle ابو المحامد و الدنيا الدين غياث	In square شـــا عمر ٩٦١ احمد بن Pl. IX. *B. B. R. A. S.*
733	–	963	Wt. 219 S. ·7	,, but no circle.	In square شـــا ٩٦٣ احمد Pl IX.
734	—	,,	Wt. 71 S. ·5	,,	,,

Æ No.	Mint	Date	Weight and size	Obverse	Reverse
				COPPER	
735	—	962	Wt. 167 S. ·75	In dotted circle غياث ٩٦٢ الدنيا سنه والدين المجاهد ابو	In square السلطان احمد شاه Pl. IX.
736	—	963	Wt. 85 S. ·55	,, but date ٩٦٣ and no dotted circle.	,, but no square. Pl. IX.
737	—	965	Wt. 173 S. ·7	,, but date ٩٦٥	,,
738	—	,,	Wt. 172 S. ·6	,,	,,
739	—	961	Wt. 172 S. ·65	الوهن بالله المعتصم و الدنيا الدين	As on No. 718, but in circle. Pl. IX.
740	—	,,	Wt. 143 S. ·6	As on No. 718.	,, but in square.
741	—	962	Wt. 215 S. ·7	,,	As on No. 719, but no peaked sided square.
742	—	,,	Wt. 213 S. ·65	,,	,, Pl. IX.

COPPER

Æ No.	Mint	Date	Weight and size	Obverse	Reverse
743	—	962	Wt. 165 S. ·6	As on No. 739.	As on No. 739, but date ٩٦٢
744	—	,,	Wt. 143 S. ·6	As on No. 718.	As on No. 741.
745	—	,,	Wt. 72 S. ·5	,,	,,
746	—	,,	Wt. 67 S. ·45	,,	,,
747	—	963	Wt. 217 S. ·7	,,	As on No. 724.
748	—	,,	Wt. 172 S. ·6	As on No. 739.	As on No. 739, but date ٩٦٣
749	—	,,	Wt. 140 S. ·65	As on No. 718.	,,
750	—	,,	Wt. 68 S. ·6	,,	,,

Æ No.	Mint	Date	Weight and size	Obverse	Reverse
					COPPER
751	—	964	Wt. 218 S. ·65	As on No. 718.	In square with peaked sides. As on No. 718, but date ٩٦٤
752	—	,,	Wt. 169 S. ·65	As on No. 739.	As on No. 739, but date ٩٦٤
753	—	,,	Wt. 140 S. ·6	As on No. 718.	As on No. 751.
754	—	,,	Wt. 143 S. ·6	,,	As on No. 752, but date ٩٦٤ like this ٩٢४; last figure being in Hindi characters. Pl. XI.
755	—	,,	Wt. 72 S. ·5	,,	As on No. 752.
756	—	965	Wt. 221 S. ·7	,,	As on No. 726. Pl. IX.
757	—	,,	Wt. 218 S. ·65	,,	As on No. 741, but date ٩٦٥
758	—	,,	Wt. 175 S. [illegible]	As on No. 739.	As on No. 739, but date ٩٦٥

COPPER

Æ No.	Mint	Date	Weight and size	Obverse	Reverse
759	—	965	Wt. 170 S. ·6	As on No. 718.	As on No. 758 Pl. IX.
760	—	,,	Wt. 163 S. ·65	,, but in scalloped circle.	,,
761	—	,,	Wt. 142 S. ·6	As on No. 718.	As on No. 742, but date ٩٦ع in this form ٩٢ع
762	—	,,	Wt. 72 S. ·5	Illegible.	As on No. 758, but date ٩٦ع in this form ٩٦ج
763	—	,,	Wt. 64 S. ·5	As on No. 718.	As on No. 758.
764	—	966	Wt. 218 S. ·6	,,	As on No. 741 but date ٩٦٦
765	—	,,	Wt. 176 S ·6	Illegible.	,, but date in this form ٩٢٢
766	—	,,	Wt. 143 S. ·55	As on No. 718.	As on No. 764.

Æ No.	Mint	Date	Weight and size	Obverse	Reverse
				COPPER	
767	—	967	Wt. 174 S. ·6	As on No. 739.	As on No. 742, but date ٩٦٧
768	—	967?	Wt. 81 S. ·5	,,	,,
768a	—	968	Wt. 212 S. ·75	,,	As on No. 742, but date ٩٦٨ *I. M. C. No. 101.*
768b	—	,,	Wt. 73 S. ·55	,,	,, but date ٩٦٨ *O. No. 26.*
769	—	—	Wt. 217 S. ·65	As on No. 718.	As on No. 718, but no date. P. IX.
769a	—	—	Wt. 218 S. ·65	ث و غيا الدنيا ابو المحامد الدين	,, Pl. IX. *B. B. R. A. S.*
770	—	962	Wt. 176 S. ·6	ابو المحامد و الدنيا الدين غياث	In circle السلطان احمد شاه ٩٦٢ Margin illegible.
771	—	964	Wt. 173 S. ·6	,,	,, but date ٩٦٤ Pl. IX.

Æ No.	Mint	Date	Weight and size	Obverse	Reverse
				COPPER	
772	—	964	Wt. 87 S. ·5	As on No. 770.	As on No. 771.
773	—	966	Wt. 79 S. ·55	,,	As on No. 770, but date ٩٦٦
774	—	968	Wt. 177 S. ·65	,,	,, but date ٩٦٨ in this form ٩٢٨
775	—	96x	Wt. 81 S. ·6	,,	,, but date ٩٢x i.e. ٩٦x
776	—	965	Wt. 176 S. ·65	,,	In circle السلطان احمد شاه ٩٦٥
777	—	,,	Wt. 167 S. ·65	,,	,,
778	—	966	Wt. 173 S. ·65	,,	In circle السلطان احمد شاه ٩٦٦
779	—	,,	Wt. 82 S. ·55	,,	,,

Æ No.	Mint	Date	Weight and size	Obverse	Reverse
					COPPER
780	—	(9)67	Wt. 174 S. ·65	As on No. 770.	As on No. 778, but date (۹)۶۷
781	—	968	Wt. 85 S. ·6	,,	,, but date ۹۶۸ Pl. IX.
782	—	967	Wt. 173 S. ·6	ابو المحامد دین و الدنیا الد غیاث	In circle السلطان ۹۶۷ احمد شاه ᛘ M. M. below mim. of Ahmad. Pl. IX.
783	—	,,	Wt. 86 S. ·55	,,	,, but no M. M.
783a	—	968	Wt. 177 S. ·6	,,	,, but date ۹۶۸ *A. N. S. No. 185.*
784	—	967	Wt. 175 S. ·65	,,	In circle السلطان شاه احمد ۹۶۷ Pl. IX.
785	—	,,	Wt. 82 S. ·55	,,	,,
786	Ahmed-ābād ?	—	Wt. 217 S. ·7	ابو المحامد غیاث و الدنیا الدین	In square شاه احمد *Margins:—* Top احمد Left آباد

Æ No.	Mint	Date	Weight and size	Obverse	Reverse
				COPPER	
787	(Ahmed) ābād	xx2	Wt. 218 S. ·7	الدنيا غيات xx۲ والدين	In square شاه احمد Left margin آباد M. M. above د of احمد Pl. IX.
788	—	963	Wt. 63 S. ·55	,, but date ۹۶۳	As on No. 786, but no margin.
788a	—	(9)63	Wt. 200? S. ·7	,,	,, *Gad. Coll.*
789	— (Shahr-i-) Mu'azzam	x64	Wt. 218 S. ·6	As on No. 787, but date (۹)۶۴	As on No. 786, but right margin المعظم
790	(Ahmed) ābād	964	Wt. 140 S. ·6	,,	,, but Left margin آباد
791	—	,,	Wt. 68 S. ·45	,,	As on No. 788.
792	—	(9)65	Wt. 217 S. ·65	,, but date (۹)۶۵	As on No. 790, but no margin.

Æ No.	Mint	Date	Weight and size	Obverse	Reverse
				COPPER	
793	—	(9)65	Wt. 138 S. ·6	As on No. 792	As on No. 788.
794	—	,,	Wt. 71 S. ·5	,,	,,
795	—	—	Wt. 71 S. ·5	الدنيا غياث	,, Pl. IX.
795a	—	—	Wt. 149 S. ·7	As on No. 787, but no date.	In double square السلطان شاه احمد ه *I. M. C. No. 102.*
796	—	—	Wt. 71 S. ·5	الدنيا غياث والدين	السلطان احمد ه شاه Pl. IX.

MUZAFFAR SHĀH, III.

Æ No.	Mint	Date	Weight and size	Obverse	Reverse
				GOLD	
AV **796a**	—	970	Wt. 185 S. ·7	In scalloped circle الرحمن المويد بتائيد النصر الدنيا والدين ابو شمس	In double square السلطان شاه ٩٧٠ مظفر بن محمود Pl. IX. *N. C. 5th Ser. Vol. IV, p. 104.*
796b	—	977	Wt. 185	المويد بتائيد الرحمن النصر الدنيا والدين	مظفر شاه بن محمود شاه السلطان ٩٧٧ *Thomas No. 15, p. 353.*

AR. No.	Mint	Date	Weight and size	Obverse	Reverse
					SILVER
797	—	968	Wt. 110 S. ·7	الرحمن المويد بتائيد النصر الدنيا والدين ابو شمس	In square السلطان مظفر بن محمود ٩٦٨
798	—	969	Wt. 110 S. ·65	,,	,, but date ٩٦٩
799	—	,,	Wt. 114 S. ·85	الرحمن بتائيد المويد شمس الدنيا والدين ابو النصر	,, but in scalloped circle. Pl. IX.
800	—	,,	Wt. 118 S. ·7	,,	,,
801	—	970	,,	,,	,, but date ٩٧٠
802	—	,,	,,	,,	,, but date in reverse form.
803	—	976?	Wt. 136 S. ·7	,,	As on No. 799, but date ٩٧٦ ?
804	—	970	Wt. 73 S. ·6	,,	In square with peaked sides. السلطان مظفر شاه ٩٧٠

Æ No.	Mint	Date	Weight and size	Obverse	Reverse
				SILVER	
805	—	971	Wt. 74 S. ·6	As on No. 799.	As on No. 804. Pl. X.
806	—	972	Wt. 35 S. ·5	,,	,, but date ٩٧٢
807	—	973	Wt. 74 S. ·6	,,	,, but date ٩٧٣
808	—	974	Wt. 72 S. ·6	,,	,, but date ٩٧٤
809	—	975	Wt. 74 S. ·6	,,	,, but date ٩٧٥
810	—	976	Wt. 70 S. ·6	,,	,, but date ٩٧٦
810a	—	,,	Wt. 35.5 S. ·5	,,	,, *A. N. S. No. 268.*
811	—	977	Wt. 73 S. ·6	,,	,, but date ٩٧٧

AR. No.	Mint	Date	Weight and size	Obverse	Reverse
				SILVER	
812	—	978	Wt. 74 S. ·6	As on No. 799.	As on No. 804, but date ۹۷۸
813	—	,,	Wt. 67 S. ·65	,,	,,
814	—	979	Wt. 74 S. ·6	,,	,, but date ۹۷۹
815	—	,,	Wt. 36 S. ·5	,,	,,
816	—	980	Wt. 73 S. ·6	,,	,, but date ۹۸۰
817	Ahmed-ābād	991	Wt. 174 S. ·85	In double linear square with dots between the lines. The Kalimah لا اله الا الله × محمد رسول الله Top margin بصدق ابی بکر Right margin بعدل عمر	In double linear square with dots between the the lines ابن محمود شاه مظفر شاه ۹۹۱ السلطان Lower margin حمد آباد Pl. X.
818	—	,,	Wt. 87 S. ·6	The Kalimah	محمود + شاه مظفر شاه ۹۹۱ السلطان Pl. X.

AR No.	Mint	Date	Weight and size	Obverse	Reverse
				SILVER	
819	—	—	Wt. 142 S. ·7	Fragments of No. 797.	In circle محمود شاه مظفر شاه بن Margin illegible. Pl. X.
				COPPER	
Æ 820	Ahmed-ābād	—	Wt. 170 S. ·6	محمود شا بن مظفر شا	احمد آباد الضرب دار
821	,,	—	Wt. 85 S. ·5	,,	,, Pl. X.
822	—	968	Wt. 163 S. ·75	Fragments of No. 799.	In circle السلطان شاه شاه ۹۶۸ مظفر بن محمود
823	—	,,	Wt. 219 S. ·7	As on No. 797.	As on No. 797, but in double square.
824	—	96x	Wt. 217 S. ·7	,,	,, but date ۹۶x Pl. X.
825	—	969	Wt. 169 S. ·6	Fragments of No. 799.	As on No. 799, but in circle.
826	—	,,	Wt. 143 S. ·65	As on No. 797.	As on No. 823, but date ۹۶۹

Æ No.	Mint	Date	Weight and size	Obverse	Reverse
					COPPER
827	—	975	Wt. 176 S. ·7	As on No. 797.	In double square with sides peaked. السلطان . شاه شاه مظفر محمود ٩٧٤
828	—	,,	Wt. 173 S. ·8	,,	,,
					Pl. X.
829	—	(9)77	Wt. 172 S. ·65	,,	As on No. 822, but date (٩)٧٧
830	—	978	Wt. 100 S. ·6	,,	As on No. 825, but date ٩٧٨
831	—	97x	Wt. 88. S. ·5	,,	,, but date ٩٧x
832	—	987	Wt. 98. S. ·7	,,	,, but date ٩٨٧
833	—	988	Wt. 151 S. ·65	,,	,, but date ٩٨٨
834	—	969	Wt. 98 S. ·6	,,	As on No. 804.

Æ No.	Mint	Date	Weight and size	Obverse	Reverse
				COPPER	
835	—	979	Wt. 98 S. ·65	As on No. 797.	As on No. 804.
836	—	971	Wt. 172 S. ·8	,,	As on No. 799, but date ٩٧١. Pl. X.
837	—	97x	Wt. 88 S. ·5	Fragments of above.	,, but date ٩٧x.
838	—	,,	Wt. 68 S. ·5	,,	,, Pl. X.
838a	—	968	—	As on No. 797.	As on No. 839, below, but date ٩٦٨ *W. M. R.*
839	—	969	Wt. 87 S. ·55	,,	السلطان شاه ٦٩ مظفر ٩
840	—	,,	Wt. 143 S. ·65	الدنيا شمس ٩٦٩ والدين	In square شاه مظفر M. M. over Muzaffar. Pl. X.
841	—	(9)70	Wt. 135 S. ·7	Fragments of No. 799.	,, but No M. M.

Æ No.	Mint	Date	Weight and size	Obverse	Reverse
				COPPER	
842	—	979	Wt. 220 S. ·7	As on No. 840, but date ٩٧١	As on No. 840. Pl. X.
843	—	970	Wt. 174 S. ·6	Fragments of No. 799.	السلطان شاه مظفر ٩٧٠ Pl. X.
844	— (Shahr-i-) Mu'azzam	,,	Wt. 220 S. ·7	النصر شمس الدنيا والدين ابو	In square ٩٧٠ شاه مظفر Right margin معظم
845	Ahmed-(ābād) (Shahr-i-) Mu'azzam	,,	Wt. 144 S. ·65	,,	but Top margin احمد Pl. X.
846	— Shahr-i-	971	Wt. 146 S. ·6	As on No. 840, but date ٩٧١	In square ٩٧١ شاه مظفر Left margins شهر Pl. X.
847	—	,,	Wt. 132 S. ·65	,, but date illegible.	,, but no margin.
847a	—	970	Wt. 147 S. ·6	Fragment of No. 105 of Muhammad Shāh II's coins but شمس, in the centre.	In circle ٩٧٠ شاه مظفر Pl. X. *B. B. R. A. S.*

Æ No.	Mint	Date	Weight and size	Obverse	Reverse
				COPPER	
848	—	971	Wt. 147 S. ·65	گردون ضرب بـــاد مهرو ماه قرص	As on No. 847a, but date ٩٧١ Pl. X.
849	—	,,	Wt. 142 S. ·6	ماه قرص مهرو بـــاد الضرب گردون تابدار	,,
850	—	,,	Wt. 137 S. ·6	Cruder form of above.	,, Pl. X.
851	—	972	Wt. 141 S. ·6	As on No. 849.	As on No. 847a, but date ٩٧٢ Margin illegible.
852	—	973	Wt. 145 S. ·6	,,	,, but date ٩٧٣
853	— bād	97x	Wt. 141 S. ·65	,,	,, but date ٩٧x and in the margin باد Pl. XI.
854	—	971	Wt. 214 S. ·7	As on No. 799.	As on No. 848.
855	—	,,	Wt. 165 S. ·6	Fragments of above.	,,

Æ No.	Mint	Date	Weight and size	Obverse	Reverse
					COPPER
856	—	971	Wt. 146 S. ·65	As on No. 799.	As on No. 851, but date ٩٧١ Pl. XI.
857	—	,,	Wt. 144 S. ·65	,,	As on No. 848.
858	—	,,	Wt. 145 S. ·65	,,	,, but script different. Pl. XI.
859	Chāmpānir	977	Wt. 214 S. ·7	As on No. 847a but date ٩٧٧	چانپانیر ضرب Pl. XI.
859a	—	971		As on No. 860 below.	As on No. 853, but date ٩٧١ *W. M. R.*
859b	—	976		,,	,, but date ٩٧٦ *W. M. R.*
860	— Shahr-i-Mu'azzam	977	Wt. 174 S. ·75	شمس الدنیا و والدین	,, but date ٩٧٧ Pl. XI.
861	—	,,	Wt. 174 S. ·6	,,	As on No. 859.

Æ No.	Mint	Date	Weight and size	Obverse	Reverse
					COPPER
862	—	977	Wt. 80 S. ·6	As on No. 860.	As on No. 859.
863	—	978	Wt. 177 S. ·75	,,	As on No. 860 but date ٩٧٨ and margin illegible.
864	Ahmed-(ābād) (Shahr-i-) Mu'azzam	,,	Wt. 178 S. ·7	,,	,, but in the margin معظم احمد
865	—	,,	Wt. 145 S. ·6	As on No. 718 of Ahmad Shah III's coins.	As on No. 847a but date ٩٠٨ Pl. XI.
866	—	(9)78	Wt. 139 S. ·7	Fragments of No. 799.	As on No. 851 but date (٩)٧٨
867	—	(9)79	Wt. 145 S. ·6	As on No. 860.	As on No. 847a but date (٩)٧٩
867a	—	(9)69	Wt. 85. S. ·5	As on No. 797.	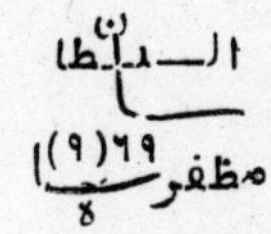 *A. N. S. No. 192.*
868	—	970	Wt. 174 S. ·6	As on No. 799.	In circle 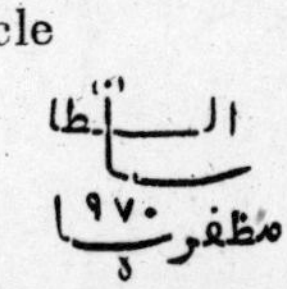

Æ No.	Mint	Date	Weight and size	Obverse	Reverse
				COPPER	
869	—	970	Wt. 172 S. ·65	As on No. 799.	As on No. 868.
870	—	,,	Wt. 85 S. ·5	,,	,,
871	—	,,	Wt. 82 S. ·5	,,	السلطا(ن) ٧٠ مظفر شا ٩ ه
872	—	971	Wt. 171 S. ·7	,,	As on No. 868, but date ٩٧١.
873	—	,,	Wt. 68 S. ·5	,,	,, Pl. XI.
873a	—	(9)79	Wt. 82 S. ·5	,,	As on No. 868, but date ٩٧٩. *Gad. Coll.*
874	—	972	Wt. 85 S. ·5	Fragments of above.	In circle ٩٧٢ Pl. XI.
875	—	(9)73	Wt. 174 S. ·55	Illegible. (٩)٧٣	In square شا مظفره

Æ No.	Mint	Date	Weight and size	Obverse	Reverse
				COPPER	
876	—	974	Wt. 175 S. ·6	Fragments of No. 799, date ۹۷۴	In circle شا مظفره
877	—	977	Wt. 172 S. ·65	As on No. 797.	In double linear square with dots between the lines السلطان ۹۷۷ شا مظفره Pl. XI.
878	—	978	Wt. 35 S. ·45	Fragments of No. 799.	۹۷۸ شا مظفره
879	—	—	Wt. 172 S. ·7	As on No. 799.	In circle السلطان شا مظفره
880	—	—	Wt. 171 S. ·7	,,	,, Pl. XI.
881	—	979?	Wt. 217 S. ·7	In dotted circle, fragments of No. 840, but date ۹۷۹ ?	In double square شا مظفره
881a	—	97x	Wt. 147·5 S. ·6	As on No. 799.	In double square السلطان ۹۷x شا مظفره *A. N. S. No. 199.*
882	—	—	Wt. 142 S. ·6	,,	In double square السلطان شاه مظفر

Æ No.	Mint	Date	Weight and size	Obverse	Reverse
				COPPER	
883	—	971	Wt. 217 S. ·75	As on No. 840, but date ٩٧١	As on No. 875.
884	—	—	Wt. 137 S. ·65	As on No. 860.	مظفر شاه السلطان Pl. XI.
885	–	—	Wt. 71 S. ·5	,,	,,
886	—	—	Wt. 129 S. ·65	,, but something below illegible.	,, Pl. XI.
886a	—	—	Wt. 137 S. ·65	شمس الدنيا والدين ابو المجاهد	,, *I. M. C. No. 117.*
887	—	—	Wt. 86 S. ·45	As on No. 799.	مظفر شاه
888	—	—	Wt. 86 S. ·55	Fragments of above.	As on No. 819, but no margin.

Æ No.	Mint	Date	Weight and size	Obverse	Reverse
				COPPER	
889	—	—	Wt. 69 S. ·5	Fragments of No. 718 of Ahmed Shāh III's coin.	In square محمود مظفر بن Pl. XI.
889a	—	982	—	Fragments of No. 799.	In circle ٩٨٢ شاه مظفر *W. M. R.*

No.	Metal.	Name of King.	Name of Mint.	Date.	Type.
				A.H.	
1	Æ	Muzaffar I ..	..	810 ..	Similar to No. 1 of this Catalogue (Pandit Ratilal of Udaipur).
2	AR	Mahmud I ..	Shahr-i-A'zam Mustafabad.	883 ..	Similar to No. 158 of this Catalogue. Schulman Sale Catalogue, 1913 (Bleazby Collection), No. 462.
3	AV	Muzaffar II ..	..	930 ..	Similar to No. 420a of this Catalogue (Bleazby Collection), No. 467.
4	Æ	"	..	919 & 923 ..	Similar to No. 479 of this Catalogue (M. K. Thakore of Broach).
5	"	"	..	..	Similar to No. 504 of this Catalogue, but weight 219 grs. (M. K. Thakore of Broach).
6	AV	Mahmud III ..	..	951 ..	Similar to No. 599d of this Catalogue. (Prince of Wales Museum).
7	Æ	Ahmad III ..	..	966 ..	Similar to No. 776 of this Catalogue (M. K. Thakore of Broach).
8	"	"	..	..	Olev : غياث الدنيا و الدين Rev : احمد بن محمود شاه 64 grs. (M. K. Thakore of Broach).
9	AR	Muzaffar III ..	..	99X ..	Similar to No. 818 of this Catalogue, but weight 44·5 gr. (M. K. Thakore of Broach).

INDEX OF MINTS.

Mint.		*Metal.*	*Date A.H.*	*Name of Sultan.*	*No. of Coin in This Catalogue.*	*Remarks.*
Ahmadabad ..	Shahr-i-Mu'azzam	Æ	910	Mahmud I ..	410	Ahmedabad or Muhammadabad.
		AR	959	Mahmud III ..	628	
		Æ	953	,,	665a	
		,,	954	,, ..	666-668	
		,,	955	,, ..	670-671	
		,,	956	,, ..	672-673	
		,,	957	,, ..	675	
		,,	960	,, ..	678a	
		,,	..	Ahmad III ..	786-787	
		,,	964	,, ..	789-790	
		,,	970	Muzaffar III ..	844-845	
		,,	977	,, ..	860	
		,,	978	,, ..	864	
,, ..	Dar-al-Zarb ..	AR	991	,, ..	817	
		Æ	..	,, ..	820-821	
Ahmadnagar ..	Shahr-i-Humayun	Æ	827	Ahmad I ..	75	
		,,	829	,,	30	
		,,	830	,,	31-32 & 76	
		,,	831	,,	33-37 & 77	
		,,	832	,,	38-39	
		,,	833	,,	40	
		,,	835	,,	74	
		,,	836		41-43	
		,,	837	,,	45-47 & 78-79	

Mint.		*Met-al.*	*Date A.H.*	*Name of Sultan.*	*No. of Coin in This Catalogue.*	*Remarks.*
Ahmadnagar ..		Æ	838	Ahmad I ..	48, 50, & 80-81	
		,,	839	,,	53 & 82-83	
		,,	840	,,	57-59 & 84-85	
		,,	841	,,	60 & 86-88	
		,,	842	,, ..	62 & 89-90	
		,,	843	,, ..	66-67 & 91-92	
		,,	844	,, ..	68 & 93	
		,,	845	,,	70 & 95-97	
		,,	846	,,	72-73 & 98-100	
Mustafabad ..	Shahr-i-A'zam ..	AR	884	Mahmud I ..	153, 158	
		,,	885	,, ..	154, 159	
		,,	886	,, ..	155, 160	
		,,	887	,, ..	163-164	
		,,	888	,, ..	156	
		,,	894	,, ..	183-186	
		,,	900	,, ..	186a	
		,,	905	,, ..	176 & 187	
		,,	906	,, ..	177-180 & 188	
		,,	909	,, ..	190	
		,,	912	,, ..	193	
		,,	913	,, ..	194	
		,,	914	,, ..	195	
		,,	915	,, ..	196	
		B	879	,, ..	325	
		,,	880	,, ..	325a	

Mint.		*Metal.*	*Date A.H.*	*Name of Sultan.*	*No. of Coin in This Catalogue.*	*Remarks.*
Mustafabad ..	Shahr-i-A'zam ..	B	881	Mahmud I ..	326-328	
		Æ	871	" ..	303	
		"	878	" ..	329a	
		"	880	" ..	304	
		"	881	" ..	305 & 331	
		"	882	" ..	306, 332, & 342	
		"	883	" ..	343	
		"	884	" ..	344	
		"	885	" ..	307, 332a & 345	
		"	886	" ..	308 & 346	
		"	887	" ..	311 & 347	
..	..	"	888	" ..	312, 348, & 350	
		"	889	" ..	314 & 349	
		"	890	" ..	315	
		"	891	" ..	316 & 351b	
		"	892	" ..	339 & 352	
		"	893	" ..	318 & 355	
		"	894	" ..	320 & 341	
		"	895	" ..	355b	
		"	896	" ..	356	
		"	899	" ..	360	
		"	906	" ..	374	

Mint.		Metal.	Date A.H.	Name of Sultan.	No. of Coin in This Calalogue.	Remarks.
Mustafabad ..	Shahr-i-A'zam ..	Æ	907	Mahmud I ..	376-377	
		,,	908	,, ..	379	
		,,	912	,, ..	391	
		AR	..	Muzaffar II ..	438	
		,,	926	,, ..	446	
Muhammadabad	Shahr-i-Mukarram..	AR	891	Mahmud I ..	202	
		,,	893	,, ..	203-204	
		,,	894	,, ..	205-210	
		,,	895	,, ..	211	
		,,	896	,, ..	212 & 227	
		,,	897	,, ..	213-214 & 227a	
		,,	898	,, ..	215-216	
		,,	899	,, ..	217-219	
		,,	900	,, ..	220 & 244	
		,,	901	,,	221,229a, & 233	
		,,	902	,, ..	222-223 & 248	
		,,	903	,, ..	224	
		,,	904	,, ..	225	
		,,	905	,, ..	226 & 228	
		,,	906	,, ..	228a	
		,,	907	,, ..	230	
		,,	908	,, ..	229	
		,,	910	,, ..	235	
		,,	911	,, ..	236	
		,,	912	,, ..	237	

Mint.		*Met-al.*	*Date A.H.*	*Name of Sultan.*	*No. of Coin in This Cata-logue.*	*Remarks.*
Muhammadabad *alias* Champaner.	Shahr-i-Mukarram..	AR	901	Mahmud I ..	245-246	
		„	902	„ ..	247 & 250	
		„	903	„ ..	251	
Muhammadabad	Shahr-i-Mukarram..	AE	905	„ ..	408	
		„	910	„ ..	410	Muhammadabad or Ahmedabad.
		AR	921	Muzaffar II ..	424a	
		„	923	„ ..	426a	
		AE	935	Bahadur Shah	579	
		„	937	„ ..	582-585	
		„	938	„ ..	586-588	
		„	939	„ ..	589-591	
		„	940	„ ..	592-593	
		„	944	Mahmud III ..	630	
Champaner ..		„	977	Muzaffar III ..	859	
Dib	Khittah	AR	900	Mahmud I ..	254-256	
		AE	..	„ ..	418	
(Dib)	Khittah	„	..	„ ..	409	
		„	..	Mahmud III ..	696a	
Burhanpur ..	..	AR	921	Muzaffar II ..	440	
		„	922	„ ..	441	
		„	923	„ ..	442	
		„	926	„ ..	442a	
		AE	920	„ ..	490a	
		„	921	„ ..	490b	
		„	922	„ ..	491	
		„	923	„ ..	492 & 492a	
Daulatabad ..	....	„	..	Mahmud III ..	704	

LEGENDS.

If we go through the mintages of the previous rulers of India, we find that it was a practice with all those monarchs to strike coins with different types and legends, and the sultans of Gujarat were no exception. If we scrutinise the list of legends, it can be seen that each sultan was striking coins with different types of legends; and the coins of Mahmud I have about twenty different varieties of legends. These legends narrate the name, the title, the faith of the ruling Sultan, and even the mint where the coins were struck. The legend on the gold and silver coins is much more elaborately designed than on the copper issues, and the full legend was stamped only on coins of the two precious metals, while on coppers the legend was only fragmentary.

The following are the different legends found on the coins of each sultan :—

1. *Muzaffar I.*

Obverse شمس الدنیا والدین

Reverse مظفر شاه السلطان

2. *Ahmad I.*

(*a*) Obverse السلطان الاعظم ناصرالدنیا والدین ابوالفتح

Reverse احمد شاه بن محمد شاه بن مظفر شاه خلد خلافت

(*b*) O. ناصرالدنیا والدین

R. احمد شاه السلطان

(*c*) O. السلطان الاعظم

R. As on previous type

(*d*) O. احمد شاه

R. السلطان

(*e*) O. ناصرالدنیا والدین ابوالفتح

R. احمد شاه السلطان

(*f*) O. السلطان الاعظم ناصرالدنیا والدین

R. As on previous type

3. *Muhammad II.*

(*a*) Obverse السلطان الاعظم غیاث الدنیا والدین

Reverse محمد شاه السلطان ابوالمحامد

(*b*) O. غیاث الدنیا والدین

R. As on previous type

(*c*) O. سکهٔ سلطان غیاث الدین محمد شاه باد

R. تا بدارالضرب گردون قرص مهر و ماه باد

(*d*) O. غیاث الدنیا والدین

R. محمد شاه السلطان

4. *Ahmad II.*

(*a*) Obverse السلطان الاعظم قطب الدنيا والدين ابوالمظفر

Reverse احمد شاه بن محمد شاه بن احمد شاه بن محمد شاه بن مظفر شاه خلد خلافت

(*b*) O. قطب الدنيا والدين ابوالمظفر

R. احمد شاه السلطان

(*c*) O. قطب الدنيا والدين احمد شاه السلطان

R. الخليفہ اميرالمومنين خلدت خلافت

(*d*) O. قطب الدنيا والدين

R. احمد شاه السلطان

5. *Mahmud I.*

(*a*) Obverse الواثق بتائيد الرحمن ناصرالدنيا والدين ابوالفتح

Reverse محمود شاه بن محمد شاه السلطان

(*b*) O. الواثق بالله المنان ناصرالدنيا والدين ابوالفتح

R. محمود شاه ابن محمد شاه ابن احمد شاه ابن محمد شاه ابن مظفر شاه السلطان

(*c*) O. ناصرالدنيا والدين ابوالفتح

R. محمود شاه السلطان

(*d*) O. السلطان الاعظم ناصرالدنيا والدين ابوالفتح

R. As on previous type

(*e*) O. السلطان الاعظم ناصرالدنيا والدين ابوالفتح

R. محمود شاه السلطان شهر مكرم محمد آباد

(*f*) O. السلطان الاعظم ناصرالدنيا والدين ابوالفتح

R. محمود شاه بن محمد شاه السلطان

(*g*) O. ناصرالدنيا والدين ابوالفتح محمد شاه

R. اخ قطب شاه بن محمد شاه السلطان

(*h*) O. ناصرالدنيا والدين ابوالفتح محمد شاه السلطان

R. الخليفہ اميرالمومنين خلد خلافت

(*i*) O. ناصرالدنيا والدين

R. ابوالفتح محمود شاه السلطان

(*j*) O. السلطان الاعظم ناصرالدنيا والدين
R. As on previous type

(*k*) O. السلطان الاعظم ناصرالدنيا والدين
R. محمود شاه بن محمد شاه السلطان

(*l*) O. ناصرالدنيا والدين ابوالفتح
R. As on previous type

(*m*) O. ناصرالدنيا والدين
R. As on previous type

(*n*) O. ناصرالدنيا والدين
R. محمود شاه السلطان

(*o*) O. السلطان الاعظم ناصرالدنيا والدين
R. As on previous type

(*p*) O. ناصرالدنيا والدين ابوالفتح
R. محمود شاه السلطان في شهر اعظم مصطفى باد

(*q*) O. ناصرالدنيا والدين ابوالفتح
R. محمود شاه بن محمد شاه السلطان (?) حمد آباد

(*r*) O. ناصرالدنيا
R. محمود شاه السلطان

6. *Muzaffar II.*

(*a*) Obverse المويد بتائيد الرحمن شمس الدنيا والدين ابوالنصر
Reverse مظفر شاه بن محمود شاه السلطان

(*b*) O. As on previous type.
R. مظفر شاه السلطان في برهانپور

(*c*) O. شمس الدنيا والدين ابوالنصر
R. مظفر شاه بن محمود شاه السلطان

(*d*) O. المويد بتائيد الرحمن شمس الدنيا والدين ابوالنصر
R. مظفر شاه السلطان خلد الله ملكه

(*e*) O. المويد بتائيد الرحمن شمس الدنيا والدين ابوالنصر
R. مظفر شاه بن محمود شاه السلطان خلد الله ملكه

(*f*) O. شمس الدنيا والدين ابوالنصر
R. مظفر شاه السلطان

(*g*) O. الموید بنا ئید الرحمن شمس الدنیا والدین
R. مظفر شاه بن محمود شاه السلطان

(*h*) O. شمس الدنیا والدین ابوالنصر
R. مظفر شاه السلطان برهانپور

(*i*) O. الموید بتا ئید الرحمن شمس الدنیا والدین ابوالنصر
R. مظفر شاه السلطان

7. *Mahmud II* (?)

Obverse ناصر الدنیا والدین ابوالفتح
Reverse ناصر شاه السلطان

8. *Bahadur Shah.*

(*a*) Obverse قطب الدنیا والدین ابوالفضل بهادر شاه بن مظفر شاه
Reverse بن محمود شاه بن محمد شاه بن احمد شاه بن محمد شاه بن مظفر شاه

(*b*) O. بهادر شاه
R. السلطان

(*c*) O. السلطان العادل
R. بهادر شاه بن مظفر شاه

(*d*) O. الموید بتأ ئید الرحمن ناصر الدنیا والدین ابوالنصر
R. بهادر شاه بن مظفر شاه السلطان

(*e*) O. As on previous type, but in place of شمس و ناصر
R. As on previous type

(*f*) O. قطب الدنیا والدین ابوالفضل
R. As on previous type

(*g*) O. بهادر شاه السلطان
R. Date in Arabic characters

(*h*) O. قطب الدنیا والدین ابوالمظفر السلطان
R. بهادر شاه بن مظفر شاه السلطان

(*i*) O. قطب الدنیا والدین
R. As on previous type

(*j*) O. قطب الدنیا و الدین
R. بهادر شاه السلطان

(*k*) O. هرکرا روی ورواج هست بر سطح زمین
R. سکهٔ اقبال شاه هند دارد بر جبین

9. *Mahmud II.*

(*a*) Obverse الواثق بالله المنان ناصر الدنیا والدین ابوالفتح
Reverse محمود شاه بن لطیف شاه السلطان

(*b*) O. ناصر الدنیا والدین
R. محمود شاه السلطان

(*c*) O. ناصر الدنیا والدین ابوالفتح
R. محمود شاه بن لطیف شاه السلطان

(*d*) O. ناصر الدنیا والدین
R. محمود شاه بن لطیف شاه السلطان मूद (मह)

(*e*) O. ناصر الدینا والدین ابوالفتح
R. محمود شاه السلطان

(*f*) O. ناصر الدینا والدین
R. محمود شاه

10. *Ahmad III.*

(*a*) Obverse المعتصم بالله الرحمن غیاث الدنیا والدین ابوالمحامد
Reverse احمد شاه بن محمود شاه السلطان

(*b*) O. غیاث الدنیا والدین ابوالمحامد
R. احمد بن محمود شاه

(*c*) O. As on previous type
R. احمد شاه

(*d*) O. As on previous type
R. احمد شاه السلطان

(*e*) O. As on previous type
R. احمد شاه بن محمود شاه السلطان

(*f*) O. غیاث الدنیا والدین
R. احمد شاه السلطان

11. Muzaffar III.

(*a*) Obverse المويد بتايدالرحمن شمس الدنيا والدين ابوالنصر

Reverse مظفر شاه بن محمود شاه السلطان

(*b*) O. As on previous type

R. مظفر شاه السلطان

(*c*) O. The Kalima

R. مظفر شاه ابن محمود شاه السلطان

(*d*) O. مظفر شاه بن محمود شاه

R. دارالضرب احمدآباد

(*e*) O, شمس الدنيا والدين

R. مظفر شاه

(*f*) O. شمس الدنيا والدين ابوالنصر

R. As on previous type

(*g*) O, تابدار الضرب گردون قرص مهرو و ماه باد

R. As on previous type

(*h*) O. مظفر شاه

R. ضرب چانپانیر

(*i*) O. شمس الدنيا والدين ابوالمجاهد

R. مظفر شاه السلطان

BIBLIOGRAPHY.

1. The Chronicles of the Pathan Kings of Delhi, by Edward Thomas, 1871.

2. Catalogue of Indian Coins in the British Museum: The Muhammadan States, by Stanley Lane-Poole, 1885.

3. Coins of the Muhammadan Kings of Gujarat, by E. E. Oliver—Journal of the Asiatic Society of Bengal, vol. LVIII, p. 1, 1889.

4. Catalogue of the Coins in the Government Museum, Lahore, by C. J. Rodgers, 1891.

5. Catalogue of the Coins Collected by C. J. Rodgers and Purchased by the Government of the Panjab, Part II: Miscellaneous Muhammadan Coins, by C. J. Rodgers, 1894.

6. Coins of the Gujarat Saltanat, by G. P. Taylor—Journal of the Bombay Branch of the Royal Asiatic Society, vol. XXI, p. 278, 1902.

7. On Some Genealogical Coins of the Gujarat Saltanat, by G. P. Taylor—Numismatic Supplement, vol. VI, 1905.

8. Catalogue of the Coins in the Indian Museum, Calcutta, vol. II, by H. N. Wright, 1907, p. 221–240.

9. Two Rare Coins of Mahmud I of Gujarat, by A. Master—Numismatic Supplement, vol. XVII, 1912.

10. A Silver Coin of Ahmad I of Gujarat, by G. P. Taylor—Numismatic Supplement, vol. XXVI, 1916.

11. Numismatic Notes (Two Silver Coins of Muzaffar Shah II), by K. N. Dikshit—Indian Antiquary, vol. XLVIII, p. 122, 1919.

12. An Unidentified Coin of Gujarat, by T. B. Horwood—Numismatic Supplement, vol. XXXVII, 1923.

13. Indian Coins Acquired by the British Museum, by J. Allan—Numismatic Chronicle, vol. IV, 5th Series, p. 103, 1924.

14. The Unpublished Coins of the Gujarat Saltanat, by S. H. Hodivala—Journal of the Bombay Branch of the Royal Asiatic Society, vol. II, New Series, p. 19, 1926.

15. The "Shah-i-Hind" Coins, by S. H. Hodivala—Numismatic Supplement, vol. XL, 1927.

16. Sultans of Gujarat, by A. Master—Numismatic Supplement, vol. XL, 1927.

17. New Types of Copper Coins of the Sultans of Gujarat, by C. R. Singhal—Indian Antiquary, vol. LVII, 1928.

18. Coins of Nasir Shah of Gujarat, by C. R. Singhal—Numismatic Supplement, vol. XLII, 1929.

19. Catalogue of the Provincial Coin Cabinet, Assam, by A. W. Botham, 1930.

20. Some New Mint Towns of the Sultans of Gujarat, by C. R. Singhal—Numismatic Supplement, vol. XLV, 1934.

COMPARATIVE TABLE OF HIJRI AND CHRISTIAN ERAS.

A.H.	A.D.	A.H.	A.D.	A.H.	A.D.
793	1390	836	1432	879	1474
794	1391	837	1433	880	1475
795	1392	838	1434	881	1476
796	1393	839	1435	882	1477
797	1394	840	1436	883	1478
798	1395	841	1437	884	1479
799	1396	842	1438	885	1480
800	1397	843	1439	886	1481
801	1398	844	1440	887	1482
802	1399	845	1441	888	1483
803	1400	846	1442	889	1484
804	1401	847	1443	890	1485
805	1402	848	1444	891	1486
806	1403	849	1445	892	1486
807	1404	850	1446	893	1487
808	1405	851	1447	894	1488
809	1406	852	1448	895	1489
810	1407	853	1449	896	1490
811	1408	854	1450	897	1491
812	1409	855	1451	898	1492
813	1410	856	1452	899	1493
814	1411	857	1453	900	1494
815	1412	858	1454	901	1495
816	1413	859	1454	902	1496
817	1414	860	1455	903	1497
818	1415	861	1456	904	1498
819	1416	862	1457	905	1499
820	1417	863	1458	906	1500
821	1418	864	1459	907	1501
822	1419	865	1460	908	1502
823	1420	866	1461	909	1503
824	1421	867	1462	910	1504
825	1421	868	1463	911	1505
826	1422	869	1464	912	1506
827	1423	870	1465	913	1507
828	1424	871	1466	914	1508
829	1425	872	1467	915	1509
830	1426	873	1468	916	1510
831	1427	874	1469	917	1511
832	1428	875	1470	918	1512
833	1429	876	1471	919	1513
834	1430	877	1472	920	1514
835	1431	878	1473	921	1515

A.H.	A.D.	A.H.	A.D.	A.H.	A.D.
922	1516	949	1542	976	1568
923	1517	950	1543	977	1569
924	1518	951	1544	978	1570
925	1519	952	1545	979	1571
926	1519	953	1546	980	1572
927	1520	954	1547	981	1573
928	1521	955	1548	982	1574
929	1522	956	1549	983	1575
930	1523	957	1550	984	1576
931	1524	958	1551	985	1577
932	1525	959	1551	986	1578
933	1526	960	1552	987	1579
934	1527	961	1553	988	1580
935	1528	962	1554	989	1581
936	1529	963	1555	990	1582
937	1530	964	1556	991	1583
938	1531	965	1557	992	1584
939	1532	966	1558	993	1585
940	1533	967	1559	994	1585
941	1534	968	1560	995	1586
942	1535	969	1561	996	1587
943	1536	970	1562	997	1588
944	1537	971	1563	998	1589
945	1538	972	1564	999	1590
946	1539	973	1565	1000	1591
947	1540	974	1566		
948	1541	975	1567		

A. TABLE OF MARKS FOUND ON THE COINS OF THE SULTANS OF GUJARAT.

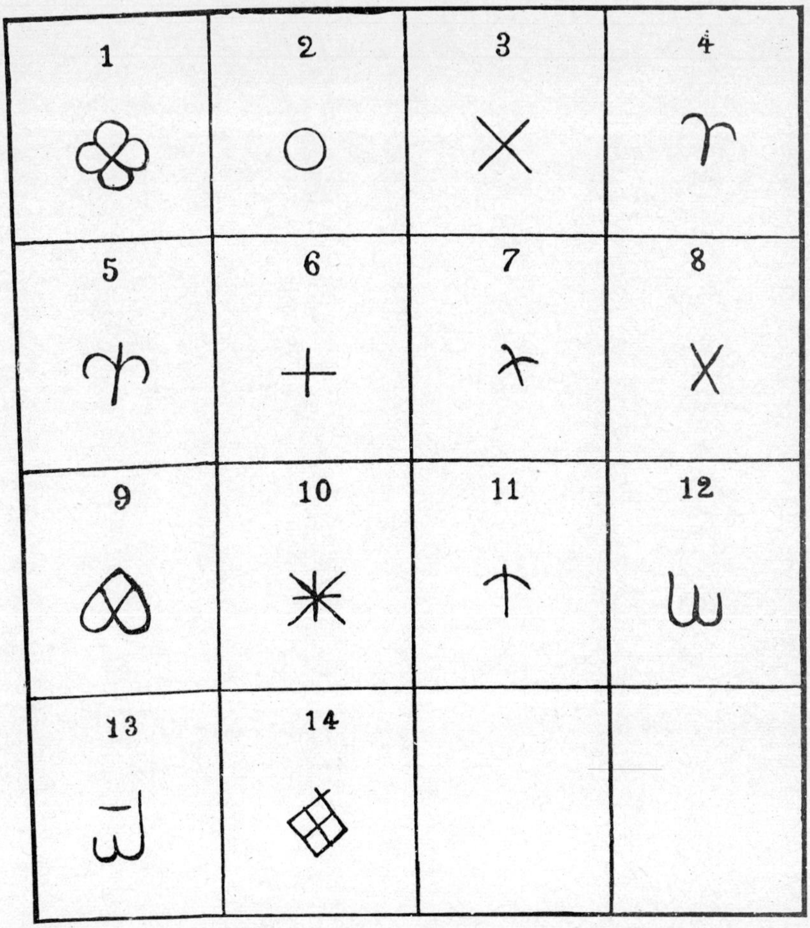

B. TABLE SHOWING COINS ON WHICH THESE MARKS OCCUR.

Mark No.	*Coin No.*	*Mark No.*	*Coin No.*	*Mark No.*	*Coin No.*
1	4, 6, & 7	5	518-521 & 525	12	840-841 & 875-876
2	4, 6, 7, 8-15, 114-115, 117, 128-142, 840-842	6	524 & 818	13	842
3	388, 523, & 817	7	632	14	853
4	517, 579-581, 583, 585, 589, 594, 782, & 787	8	663		
		9	708-709, 840, 842, & 875		
		10	711		
		11	817		

Plate I.

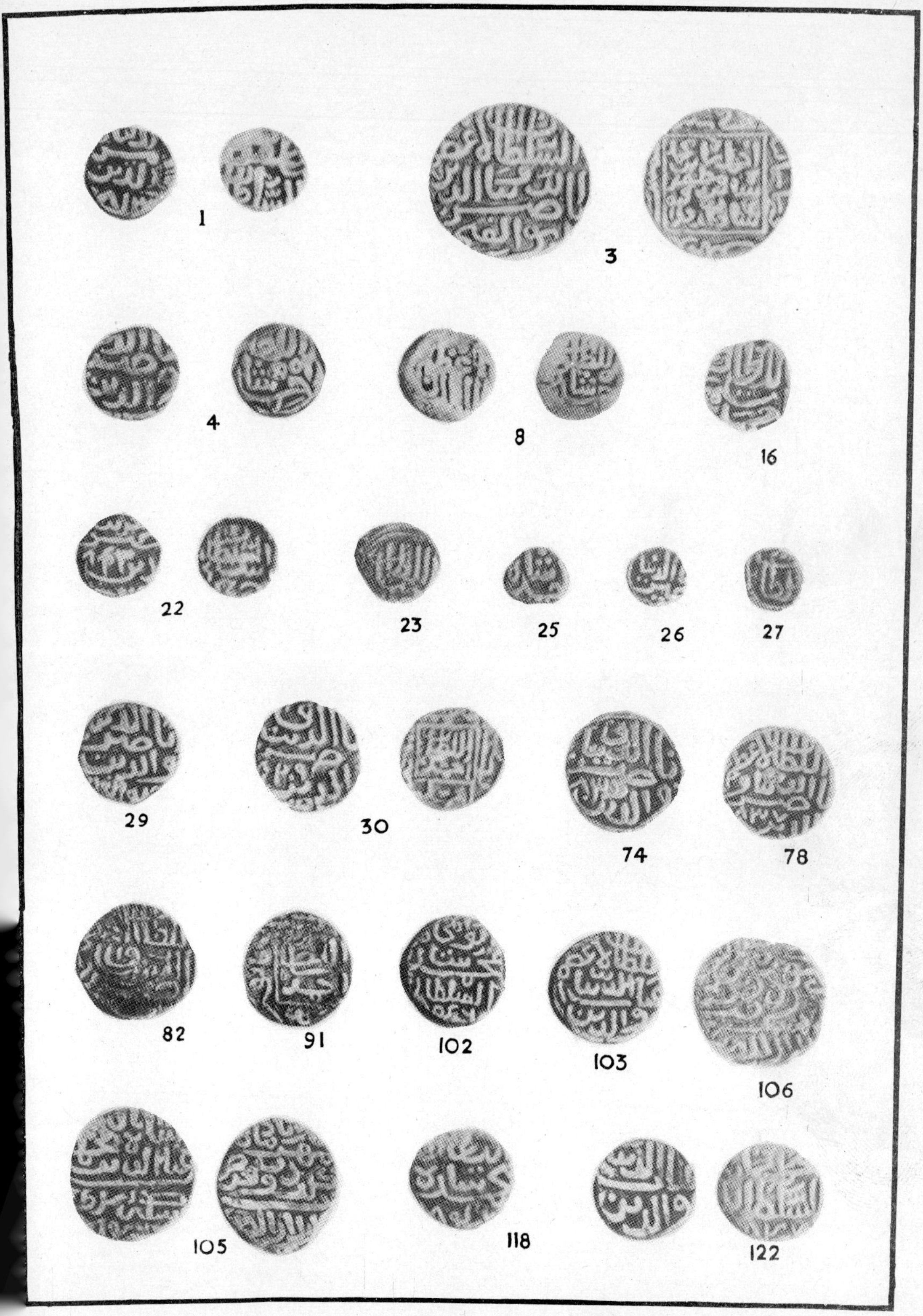

Muzaffar Shah I, Ahmad Shah I and Muhammad Shah II.
(No. 1.) (No. 3—91.) (No. 102-–22.)

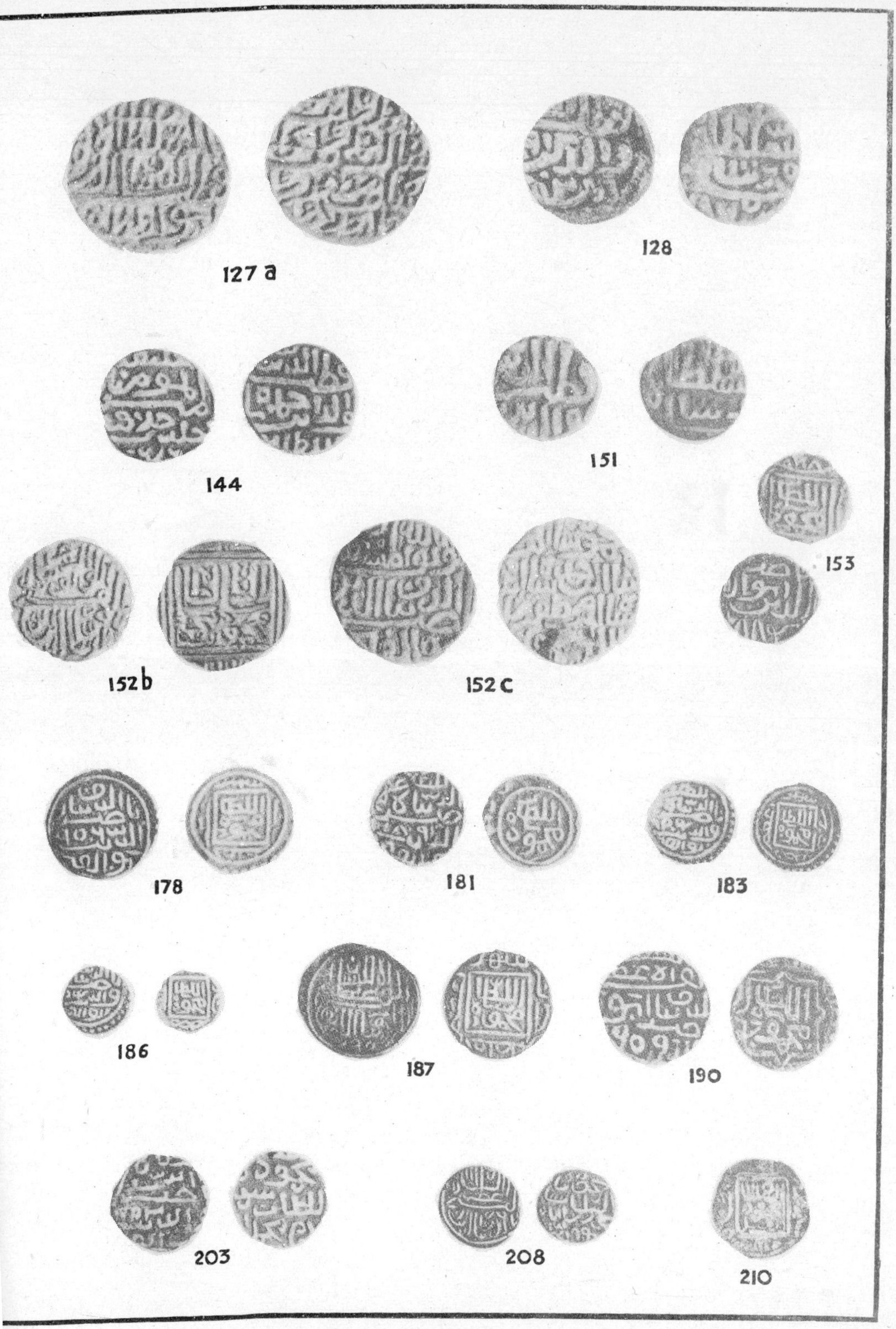

Ahmad Shah II, Mahmud Shah I.
(No. 127*a*—151.) (No. 152*b*—210.)

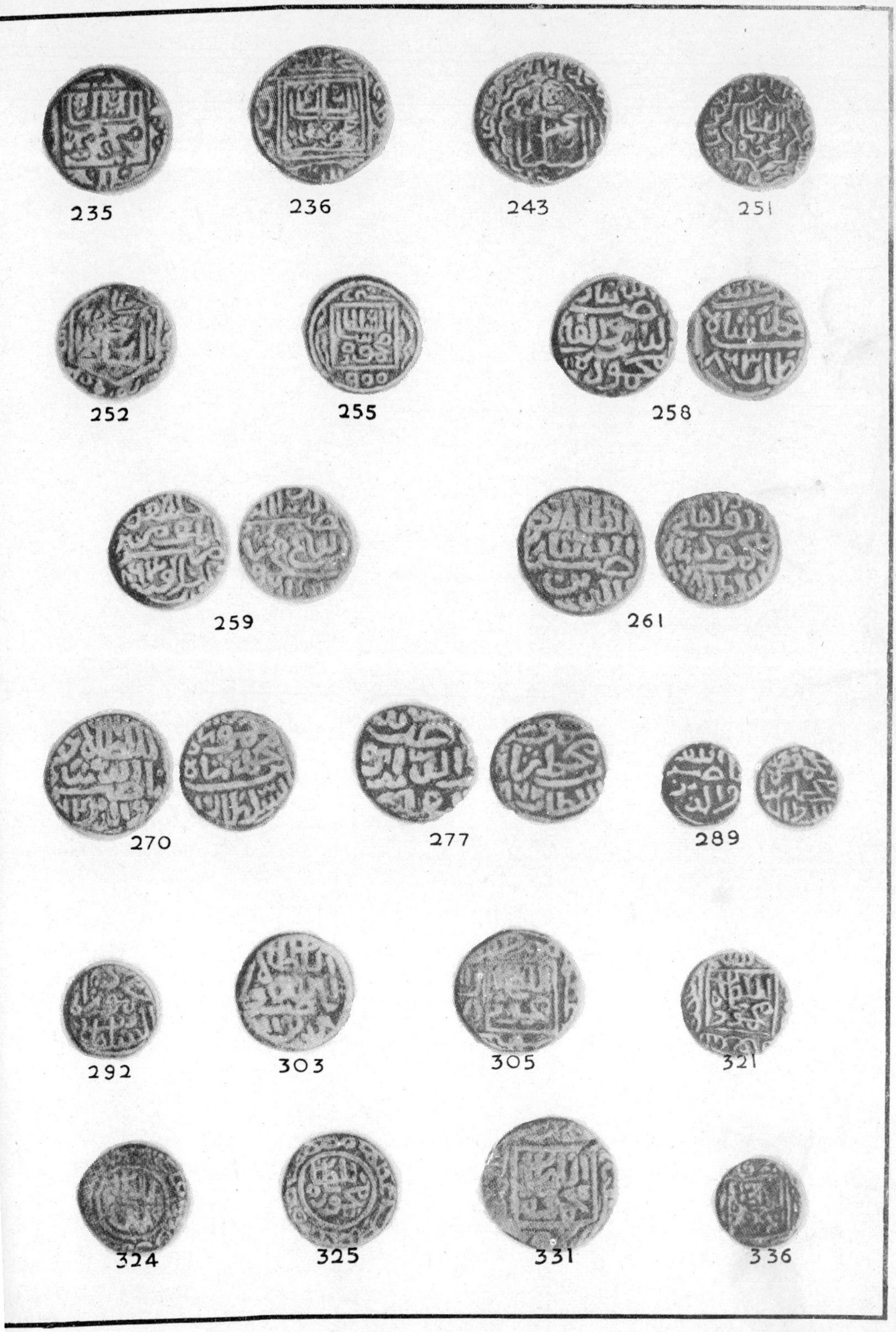

Mahmūd Shāh I.

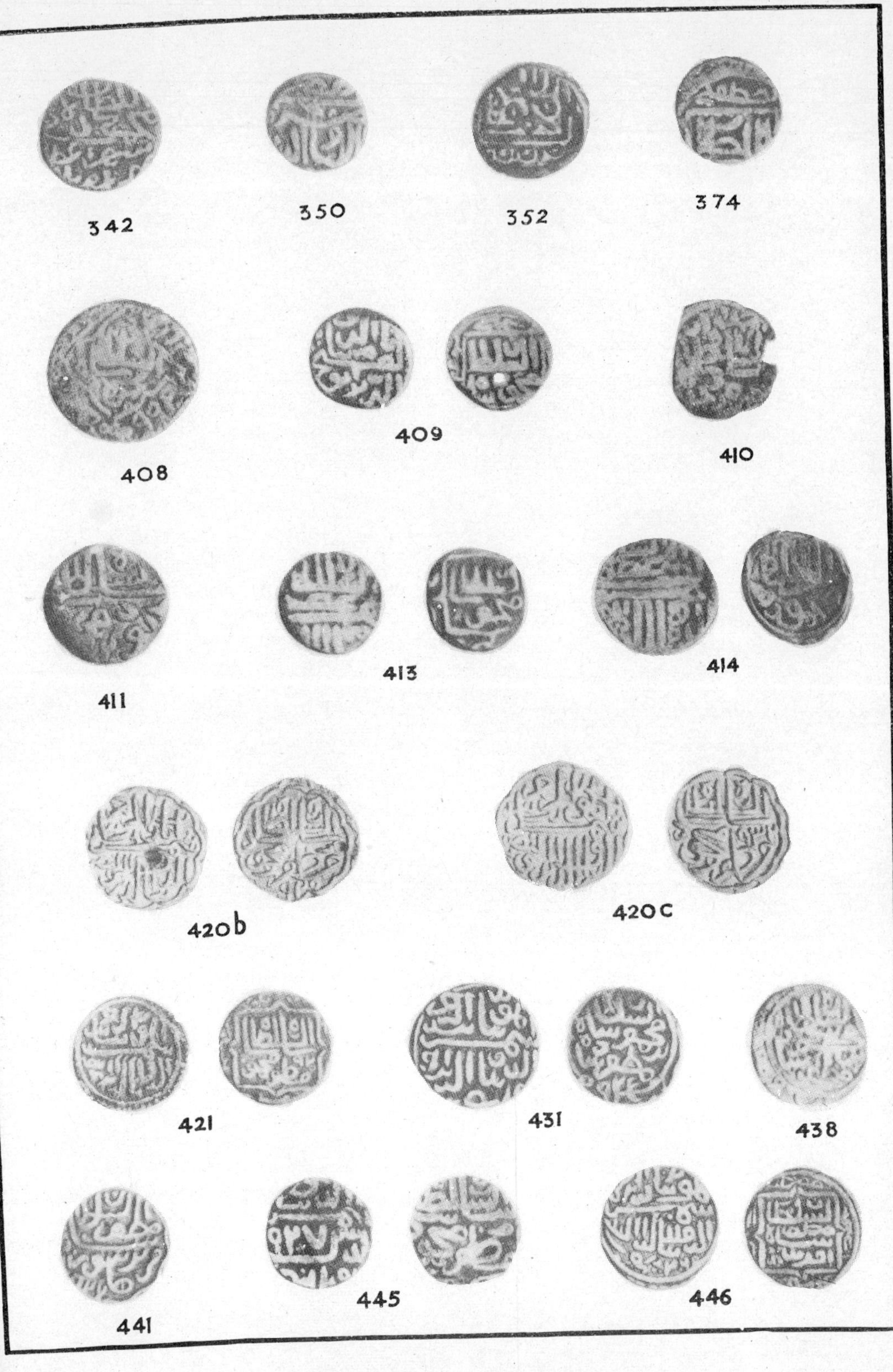

Mahmud Shah I, Muzaffar Shah II.
(No. 342—414.) (No. 420*b*—446.)

Plate V.

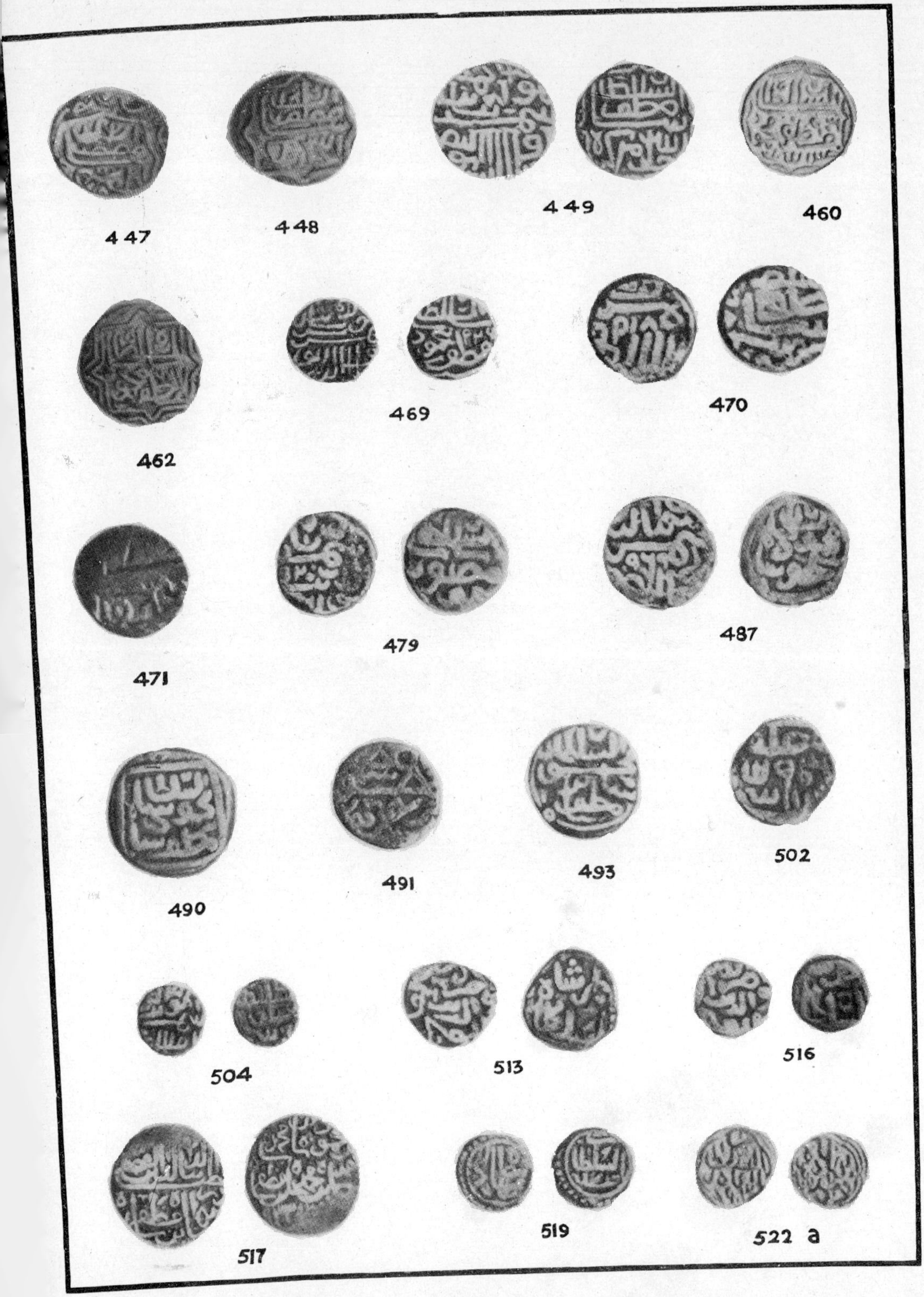

Muzaffar Shah II, Mahmud Shah II ? and Bahadur Shah.
(No. 447—504. (No. 513—16.) (No. 517—22*a*.)

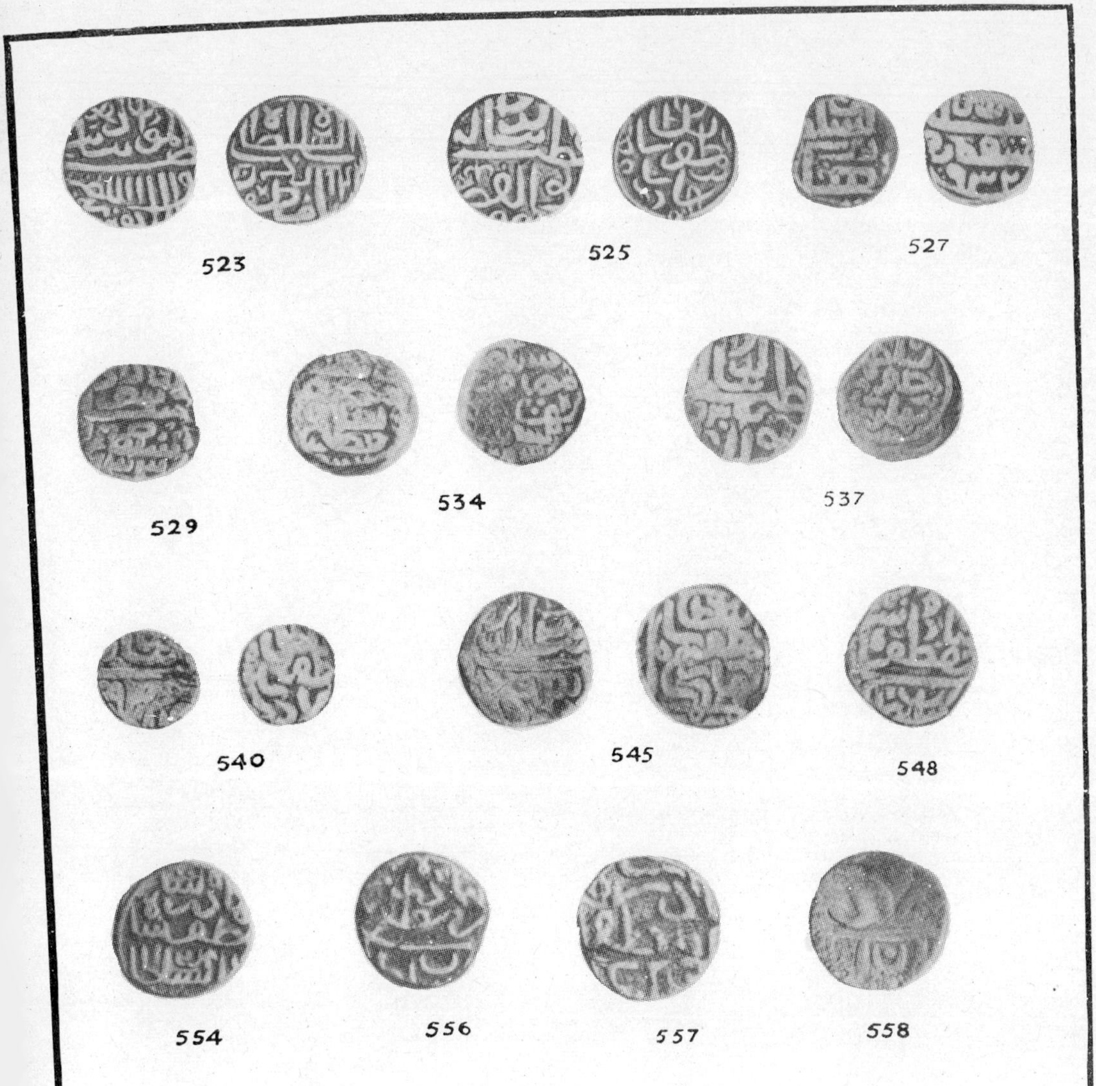

Bahadur Shah.

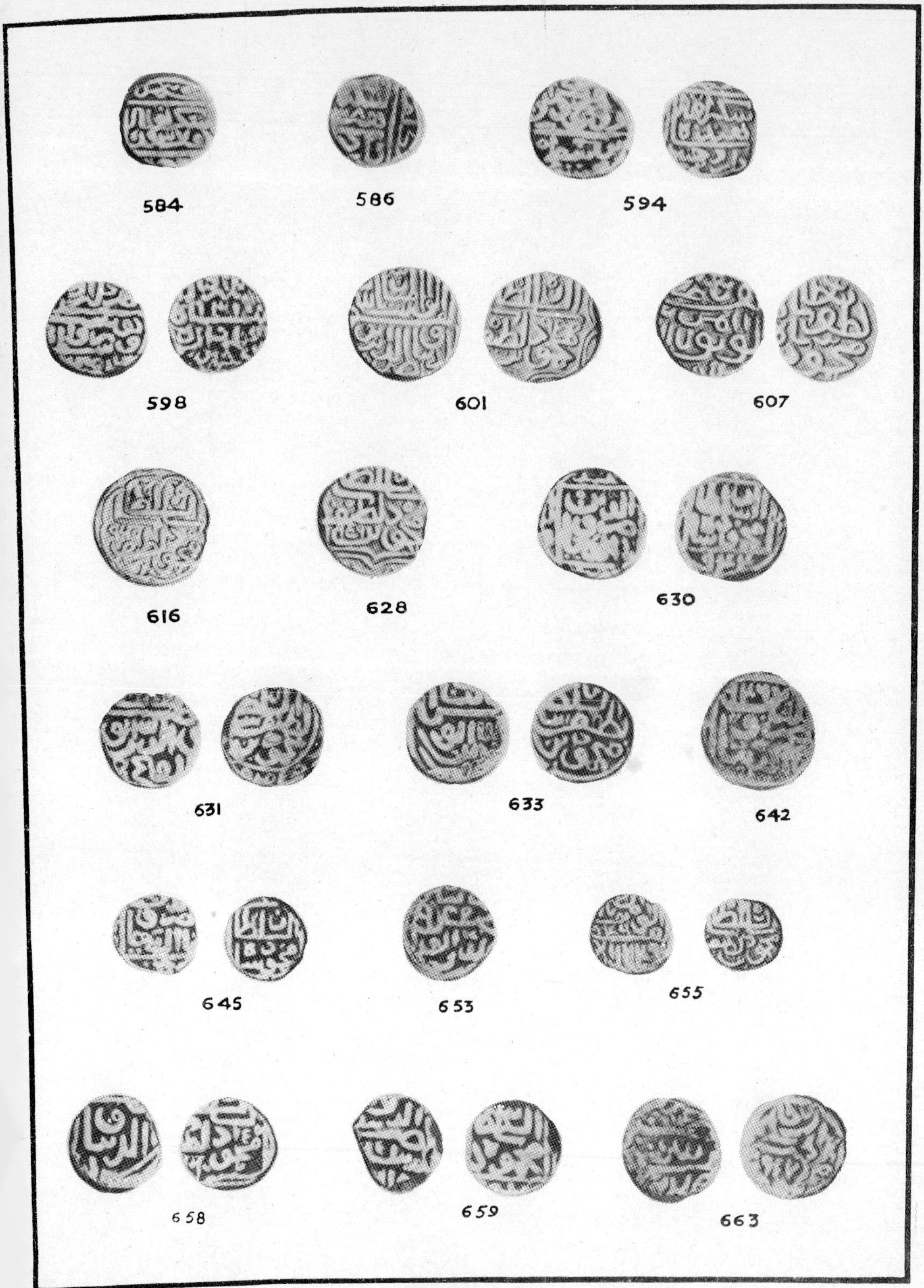

Bahadur Shah. Mahmud Shah III.
No. 584 98.) (No. 601 63.)

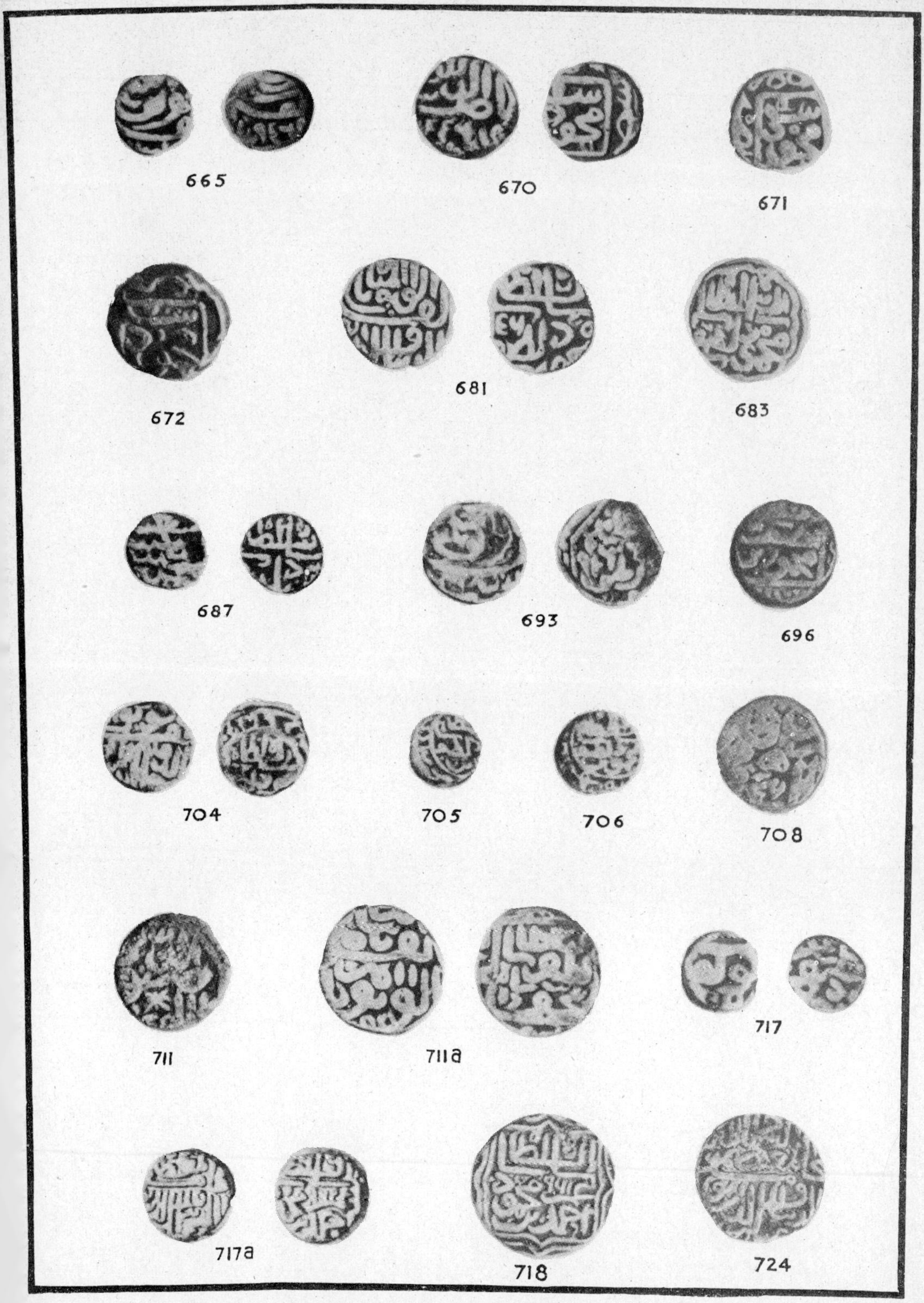

Mahmud Shah III, Ahmad Shah III.
(No. 665—717.) (No. 717*a*—24.)

Plate IX.

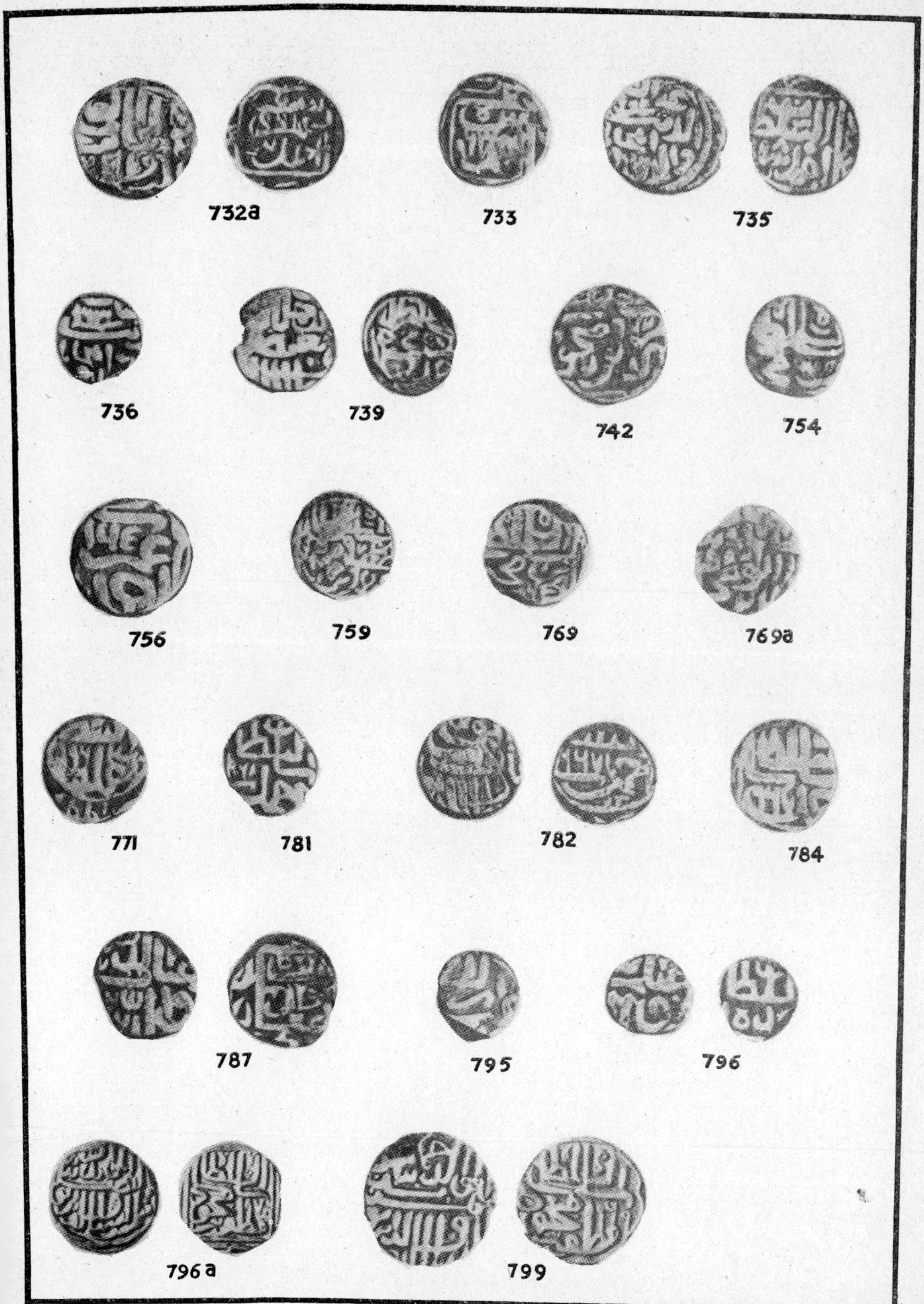

Ahmad Shah III, Muzaffar Shah III.
(No. 732*a*—96.) (No. 796*a*—99.)

Plate X.

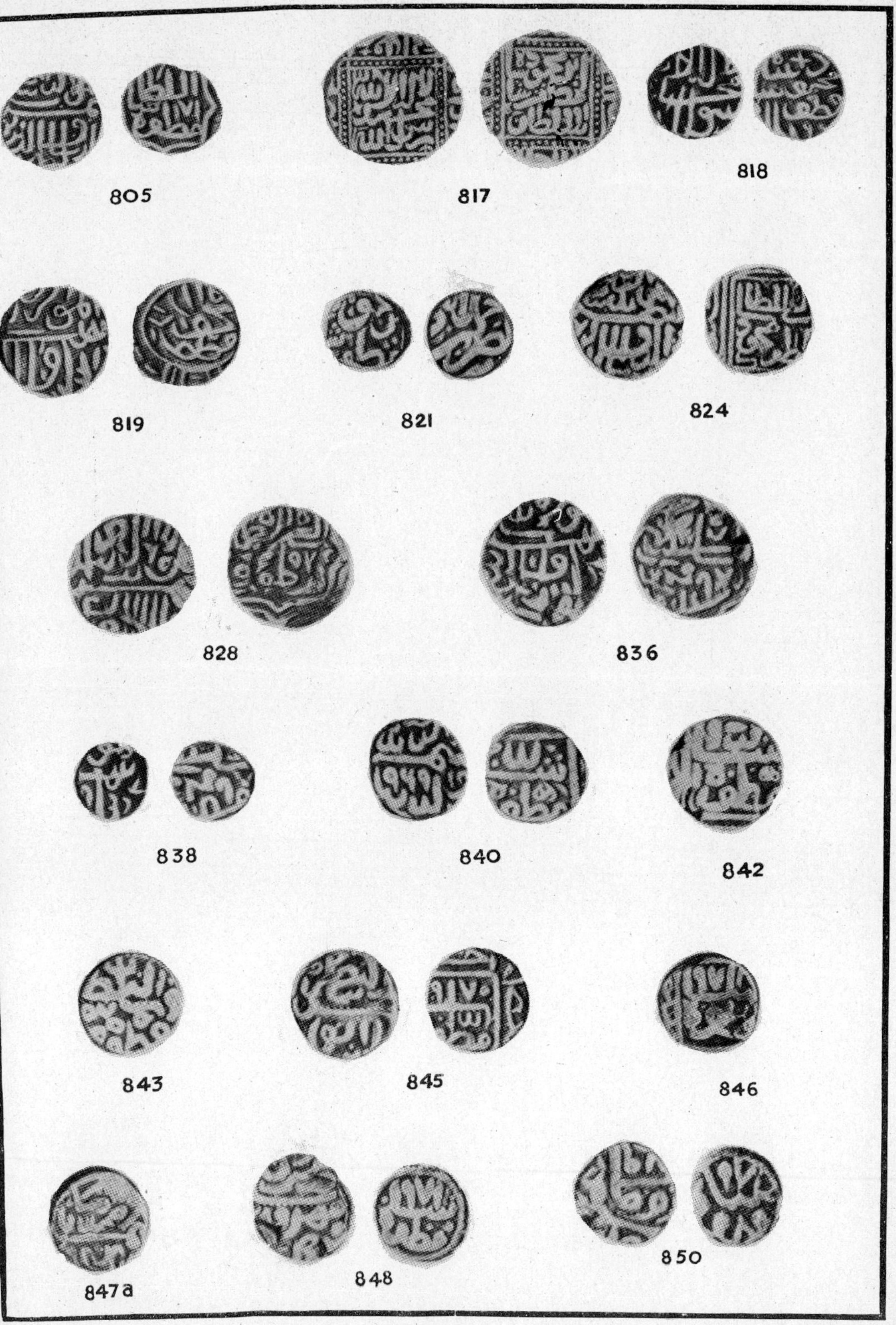

Muzaffar Shah III.

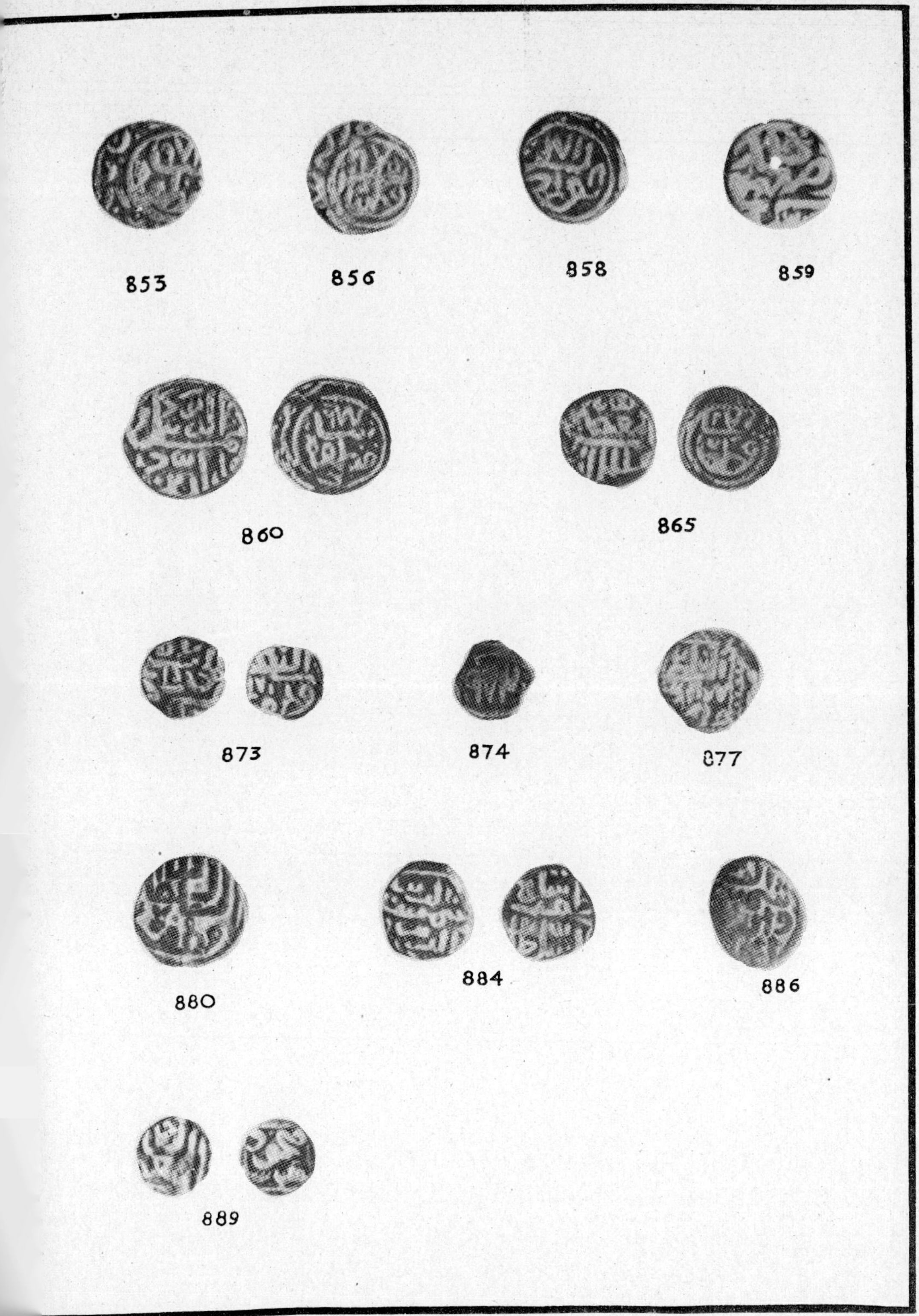

Muzaffar Shah III.